Behind the Grey Hair

Best Wishes To Carolyn

Compiled by

Jo Stichbury

LIST OF CONTRIBUTORS

1929 Joyce   Born in Newcastle under Lyme.
Teacher. Married. Has two children and two
grandchildren. Moved to Poulton. Founder member of
Fairford u3a.

1937 Rosemarie   Born in Surrey. Teacher then
Headmistress. Has a son with four children and a daughter
wifth two children. Now lives in Cirencester.

1937 Jo   Born in Walthamstow, East
London. Creative Writing teacher. Married, with two
children, five grandchildren, three great grandchildren.
Widowed and now living in Fairford.

1939 Maureen   Born in Burnley. Computer
programmer. Lives in the Cotswolds. Widowed, with two
children and two grandchildren.

1944 Jude   Born in Cosham. Lawyer in
London. Married, with two children. Now lives in
Fairford.

1960 Jocelyn   Born in Cheltenham. University
lecturer. Married, with four children. Now living in
Lechlade when not on a canal boat.

1961 Carol   Born in Croydon. Worked mainly
in Music Retail. Married. Now living in Derbyshire.

CONTENTS

INTRODUCTION

What have a group of retired ladies who live in a picturesque part of the country got to say of interest? They are just grey-haired old ladies, aren't they? Yet talk to them and you will find they have remarkable stories to tell.

Who would expect a girl born in in the 1920s to take part in a round-the-world yacht race or a woman born before the Second World War to ride a camel in the Gobi Desert at the age of seventy, as Joyce and Rosemarie did? Imagine a girl who missed the first two years of her education through tuberculosis and had to leave school at fifteen; Jo dreamed of going to university and finally achieved it at the age of sixty. Today's image of a computer programmer is that of a geeky young man, yet Maureen began a career in programming in the 1960s. Jocelyn was studying for a doctorate whilst expecting her first baby; she was printing out drafts of her thesis during early labour. If you have ever dreamed of meeting your pop idol, envy Carol who worked on the edge of the music scene and got to meet many of hers. Jude was kidnapped by gangsters and held at gunpoint overnight whilst a daring jewellery raid took place.

These don't sound like ordinary women, yet they do not consider themselves anything out of the ordinary. They are women who took whatever life threw at them and made what they could of it.

These women grew up at a time when the education of a girl was still seen by some as a waste of money. They grew up with the doctrine that a woman's place was in the home. Their persistence has opened up the world of opportunity that today's girls enjoy. The problem of work-life balance is something that the current generation struggles with, but it is not a new one. Rosemarie wrestled with it throughout her career as a Primary School Head Teacher. You have heard talk of the glass ceiling which prevents women taking up senior positions in many spheres, but no one talks about the glass door that Jude had to break down to establish a successful London Law practice. Disability is a challenge in any generation. Carol travelled the world despite a painful condition that meant she could scarcely walk on some days.

These women fought battles without even thinking about them. They protested against the nuclear arms race, went to Greenham Common, rode motorbikes and were among the first to have fathers present during childbirth. They laid the foundation for the lives that today's women take for granted. Their stories – our stories - deserve to be told.

We in the Fairford and District u3a Creative Writing Group, are recounting our lives. It is now 2022. We are a collection of seven women of varying ages who have come together to compare our lives and achievements. We have all ended up in the Cotswolds coming from all over the country. We come from various backgrounds and our lives have been so different. We have lived through a wide range of experiences and events during this twentieth century. Our years of birth range from nineteen twenty nine to nineteen sixty one and it was an eye opener to us how much has changed and also how much has not.

We looked at education, health (including childbirth), travel and personal leisure, careers, response to world events and, of course, for the older ones the impact of World War 2.

We are remembering trivia that is now history. The once ordinary is now fascinating. None of us could have done anything about being born in a particular place at a particular time or to particular parents. That was our lot and we had to make the most of it. Some of us were advantaged from the start. Others were not so advantaged but we have all struggled in our own ways to find our place in the world despite the accidents of our birth and the experiences of our early lives which so shaped us. We have absorbed. We have learned. We have laughed. We have cried. We have all sought to find our own level. We have escaped. We have survived. Different as we all are in terms of age, childhood and adult experiences, and in what we have achieved or not as the case may be, here we are today, a group of like-minded people, sharing our past lives with each other, baring our souls and finding a common purpose.

Thank you, Jo, for bringing us together and fostering such a sense of belonging to each other notwithstanding our differences.

Some names have been changed for privacy reasons.

1 FORMATIVE YEARS

Give me a child until seven…

Something like this is what we thought when starting out on this project. Our birthdates range from 1929 – 1961 so we were seven women born at different times in history. Some older ones can remember the war years and having to dive to the shelter or under the table; these were ordinary everyday occurrences. Others remember the threat of atomic warfare and the fear some felt. Countrywide strikes and power cuts, the three-day week. Although it was not all like that. 1951 brought the Festival of Britain. And gradually, travel, which nowadays is taken for granted by so many. So we started with our much different childhoods, or formative years.

Joyce   *Aged 10+(1939) My Music*

When I was young music did not feature largely in my life. We had a radio, but I always preferred to listen to the spoken word. Mother had a pleasant voice and sang Methodist hymns of which she had a large repertoire. I left the quiet ones to her and just hummed along, falling silent on the higher notes, but in Chapel even I joined in to belt out "Bread of He-ea-ven", hoping that any flat notes would be hidden by the organ.

At school we had music lessons, which consisted of class singing accompanied by the pupils who had piano lessons. We had a ghastly tuneless school song which began "Nunc canendum, nunc laetandum..." I never knew what it meant, since I had opted for German instead of the 'dead' language. I was once foolish enough to ask the music teacher who the composer was. I was not a bit surprised when she said that SHE had composed it. The trouble was that she enquired why I had asked. I could hardly say what I was thinking, so I mumbled something about "just wondering", and learned to keep my mouth shut.

Why I joined the school choir I can't imagine, but there was no audition so I enjoyed squeaking my best to "Sheep may safely graze" and "The Skye Boat Song." I loved the melodies so when I had started to work I paid to have piano lessons from the teacher across the road. I was so keen that I bought a £10 piano and persuaded my long-suffering mother to house it, wedged behind the door in our tiny front room. I was no more adept at piano than I had been at singing, but I enjoyed playing simplified versions of popular classics.

By the 1940's I was living in Newcastle-Under-Lyme, where we had an Anderson shelter at the bottom of our garden. I lived in Newcastle until I was about sixteen. Then a disturbing thing happened, my parents split up. Mother left with us kids. We did not move too far, a room in a cousin's house at Stoke on Trent. One abiding memory for me was the steelworks. At night the glow from these works lit up the sky and could be seen from quite a distance.

When I was seventeen, I left home to go to a teacher training college. On reflection the training was very limited, two years basic, plus an extra year so that I could go straight from that to a secondary school to teach.

In nineteen seventy one I was one of the first students at the Open University. It was very experimental at the beginning. We students were trail blazers really. The O.U. was trying out different systems with a completely new and different subject each month. I remember the first month was Astronomy. I thoroughly enjoyed that as an introduction to such a new subject. I was there for three years, after which I ended up teaching in Rugby.

BEHIND THE GREY HAIR

Rosemarie   *1937 to 1955*

It was a home birth, with the district nurse in attendance. She called at the house regularly until I started school.

My mother was a housewife, my father a white-collar worker. We lived in a village near Farnham in a semi-detached house on an unmade road near a copse. There were open fires, gas lighting and one cold water tap. There was a gas cooker.

I was an only child. My parents' first child, a boy, died aged eight months before I was born.

My earliest memories are of sleeping in a cot, being pushed in a pram, and visiting my paternal grandfather whom I adored. These events happened before my third birthday.

Milk was delivered by horse and cart. Dustmen came weekly in a lorry. Coal was delivered in hundredweight sacks. Bread was bought from the baker in the village. If a convoy was going through, pedestrians had to wait for it to pass before crossing the road. I went on my own to buy the bread from the time I was five, crossing the road. There were few private cars, and in the road where I lived no-one owned a car. At some point during the war petrol was rationed which meant even less traffic.

I was a fussy eater and underweight. My mother bought goats' milk for me. I was brought up during wartime food rationing. My mother preserved runner beans in an earthenware pot, each layer covered with salt. Eggs were preserved in isinglass. Fruit was bottled in kilner jars which had rubber sealing rings. She made jam with any fruit available, which included blackberries in season.

The meat at Christmas dinner was chicken which would have started life as a chick in the garden. An uncle wrung its neck when the time came, as my dad refused. Christmas cake, mincemeat and Christmas pudding were home-made. The puddings were boiled for a minimum of six hours to give them a rich colour. The cake in its tin was wrapped with newspaper to ensure slow cooking which took several hours. The mincemeat ingredients were put through a hand turned mincer which was clamped to the kitchen table. This mincer was also used throughout the year to put through cooked meat, the process being finished with a slice of bread to ensure no meat was wasted. The bread also padded out the amount of meat when meat rationing meant a minimal amount per person per week.

I remember an air raid shelter being installed in the garden. My grandmother came to live with us in about 1940. In due course my Dad was conscripted into the army and served at the end of the Italian campaign.

There was a pottery near our house. I used to watch the pots being thrown on a wheel. Near the pottery was a storage tank of water, a reserve should there be an interruption to the regular supply to local houses.

My first experience of school was 'Sunday school' in a chapel near home. My neighbour attended a service there on a Sunday and I went with her, but into the school room. I loved the hymn-singing and the stories. We learned just a few hymns. The neighbour gave me a Children's Bible for Christmas, but it was extracts from The Holy Bible covering biblical stories such as Daniel in the Lions' Den. The language was far too difficult for me. In due course I stopped Sunday School and went to church, Matins with my mother, there being no Sunday School at that church.

I started main-stream school the term after my fifth birthday. It was a one form entry infant school There were three classes. My first teacher was Mrs Skillen. I liked school and the routine. The tables were arranged in long rows facing the front. The blackboard was on an easel which would now be a health and safety hazard but caused no problems, since once seated we did not move around. One day I was promoted to sit on the far right of the front row as I was deemed a star pupil. This was because I had quickly taken to learning. The basic lessons were reading, writing and sums (not called mathematics when I was that age). I was weak at spelling. I remember playing a triangle in music lessons.

In the middle class there were desks with two children to a desk and in the top class there were tables arranged in squares, an innovative Head I think.

By aged seven we were expected to know our times tables up to twelve times twelve, a table about weight, such as fourteen pounds equal one stone, a table about money, such as two hundred and forty pennies make a pound, and measurement of distance, such as twenty two yards equal one chain.

There was a mid-morning and mid-afternoon break. There was a third pint of milk per child per day drunk at morning playtime. Haliborange was also provided and this I had at home, a spoonful a day to ward off colds. Lunch, called dinner, was an hour and a half and most children, including me, had time to go home for dinner, the main meal of the day.

All meals at home were taken at a table covered with a white cloth. This and all other washing was done by hand. My mother had two flat irons that were heated on the gas stove. One would be in use. When it cooled off it would be swapped for the other. To test the heat, she upended the iron and spat on it. If the spital shot across the room, it was hot enough to use. If it sizzled the iron was put back on the stove to heat more.

At the end of the school year in which I was seven I went to Junior School, an old church school building on the same site separated by fencing. A pot -bellied stove in each classroom provided warmth. There was a gradual influx of evacuees and class sizes swelled to 42 to 48 per class.

I joined the Brownies. I was in the Pixie six. I loved the badge work and earned a 'Golden hand' after a set number of badges.

There was an air raid shelter in the school grounds. I went in there just once. I could identify some aircraft by sound.

The lavatories were at the end of the playground away from the school. The playground was divided into two, boys one side, girls the other. In the playground we played clapping games, cat's cradle, skipping, whip and top, 'he' and a number of other chasing games of our own creation.

There was a school library and books could be exchanged weekly. I loved Enid Blyton's Famous Five and her mystery stories. I also read Angela Brazil, graduating to Heidi by aged eleven.

There was a trainee teacher at one point, a Mr Richardson, on a one-year training programme. He taught us maths. He drew a circle on the blackboard and called it his apple pie. He had rapport, made us laugh and his ability to teach fractions as he divided his apple pie, I still remember.

Of the other staff, the school secretary had been widowed when her sailor husband died on board his ship in the Mediterranean, leaving her with three young children. One class teacher lost her brother, father and fiancé, all sailors, whilst two others were widowed. These had a mention in morning assembly, but I do not recall them being off work for more than a day or two. One temporary teacher came from Portsmouth to the area. She had lost half her class in a bombing. She was bad-tempered and I was scared of her.

A teacher taught us how to knit fair isle. Post war there was a school play in the village hall. I was a robin. There was a trip to London and one to Portsmouth.

There was no school uniform at either infant or junior school. In the infants I wore cotton dresses in summer and skirts and hand knitted jumpers in winter. I had a woollen coat and a pixie hood, the latter knitted as a rectangle which was then sewn up along one side to form a hat. Underwear was vest, knickers and liberty bodice. At junior level the liberty bodice was not worn. A knitted beret, often in fair isle, replaced the pixie hood. I usually wore a cardigan over a summer dress. There were clothing coupons, a form of rationing, and some of my clothes came from a clothing exchange where children's clothes could be swapped cost and coupon free.

Leather shoes with a bar across were worn in winter and white canvas shoes the same shape in summer. The white canvas was cleaned with blanco. A big treat was having the toes cut out of the canvas shoes as I grew to make 'toe out' sandals but for home wear only.

On VE day I was staying with relatives in Southampton. We walked into town and danced in the streets.

Shortly before my eleventh birthday I was told that I had passed the 'eleven plus', an exam that enabled me to go to the local girls' Grammar School. A letter arrived with a list of uniform needs plus a bus pass. The school leaving age had been raised to fifteen, but sixteen if you went to Grammar School, and eighteen if you planned to go into further education.

The uniform was a navy pinafore dress and white winceyette blouse in winter and spring and blue cotton dress in summer. There was a blazer with school logo and a beret. Additionally, a satchel was needed plus tennis racket, hockey stick and PT kit of pale blue aertex shirt and navy blue knickers and plimsoles.

On the first morning I walked to the bus stop five minutes from home, getting off at the stop nearest the school which meant a twenty-minute walk. There were no school buses.

It was a two-form entry. On the first morning we went into the hall and were told which class to go to. The classrooms had desks in rows facing the blackboard, two pupils per desk. Once in class we had a timetable for lessons and which rooms to go to. It was completely different to Primary School as it was a different teacher for each subject and different rooms for example for music, maths, geography, art, science and PT (Physical Training later known as PE for Physical Education).

Teachers delivered lessons and set homework. There was no interaction between pupils and staff, hence no guidance on how to improve. There were subjects in which I was strong but in others I fell foul of the system.

In the first two years two of my best friends left the school relocating to different parts of the country. Inevitably there were class bullies. My first two years were not happy though I did enjoy being in a school play. Perhaps I was changing and it was all part of puberty and growing up. I had school dinners daily and they were good. There was a tuck shop at break time.

Another memory of school includes a trip to the Festival of Britain. One lunch time the Headmistress (note: not Headteacher) came into the dining hall to say King George VI had died.

I joined the Guides and went on Guide camp which I thoroughly enjoyed but I left Guides after a year.

My grandmother, who had lived with us, died when I was twelve. My parents started house hunting and we moved into a bigger house with a reasonable garden when I was about thirteen. It was on the edge of Farnham and I could walk into town. I cycled to school. My father bought a car. I remember a holiday in the lake district. I had a camera and got up early to snap the reflections in a lake while all was totally still. We always had one seaside holiday a year. Farnham was twinned with a Dutch town and I had a holiday there staying in a private house.

An Uncle used to take my parents and me to Southsea after tea once or twice a week and we would swim then come home. I loved doing that.

I was confirmed, when I was fourteen, in the Church of England and joined a church youth club. A neighbour was a bell ringer and I learned to ring at St. Andrews' Farnham, beginning when I was fifteen. Life opened up. There were ringing outings some Saturdays to different areas where we rang, known as tower grabbing. I cycled to practice nights in Aldershot and Ash, plus going to Farnham practice nights, so three evenings a week I was out. Boy friends came on the scene. I joined a different youth club. I was bridesmaid to a cousin.

On the day of the coronation of Queen Elizabeth the second I went to a neighbour to watch it on television. There was no television at home though we had one not long after that. Rationing came totally to an end when I was sixteen.

With sixteen approaching I had to decide on a job. My father arranged for me to spend three days in a bank, where I learned that the first two years at least would have to be spent 'backstage' before there would be any hope of being a cashier. A cashier would be the pinnacle of achievement for, if there were women managers or deputy managers, I never heard of them.

Comptometer operator was also considered but a day or two work-shadowing convinced me that office work, including the bank, was claustrophobic and not for me. I must stay on at school.

Now the school was a bit helpful. The Headmistress idolised those aspiring to go to university. A 'State scholarship' was awarded to star pupils which was a considerable help with fees for those going to university. I declined that route. I wanted to be a primary school teacher, which meant training college. The advice from the school was to take five GCSE subjects one year then five more the next, as a broad range was needed by primary school teachers. This left one year to study A-level but not enough time to do an A-level course for an exam. I did English and French. I also did Book-Keeping as an extra.

I played hockey for the school in the winter and threw the javelin in the summer. I was in a school play, Quiet Weekend, which was a collaborative effort with the drama group from the local boys' Grammar School, innovative indeed.

Post sixteen, the school recommended applying to certain training colleges according to their rating. The top ones had a tick in the box for each of the following: a) their high reputation and hence a good chance of getting a job at the end of the two years b) their pass rate success (I chose one with a 96% pass rate) and c) the opportunities for course work and recreational studies which they offered. Homerton Students' Union was part of the Cambridge Student Union group, which attracted many, but I applied to Bishop Otter Training College in Chichester and was accepted.

During my final year at school I had a Saturday job in a Sports shop.

Boys at that time had to decide when to do National Service i.e. on leaving school then go to university, training college or whatever their chosen path, or whether to do their training first then National Service. For those becoming doctors or engineers this meant going into the services five to seven years after leaving school. Girls did not have to do National Service.

There was a party at home for my eighteenth birthday for relatives, and also one for friends. The real celebrations would be when I was twenty-one. I left school just after my eighteenth birthday. My mother took a picture of me when I arrived home. I remember feeling excited about the future.

Jo   *1937 to 1960*

29.11.37

I was born in Walthamstow, Mum and Dad lived in a 'Warners' flat. These were flats owned by a company in the area. I must admit I do not remember this at all. Apparently Uncle Bill (mum's brother,) died in the same year.

1940

My sister Carole was born 27.8.1940 and my Grandad, my Mum's father, died.

It is hard to remember exact dates. I know Carole was with us at Weston-Super -Mare as I have photographic evidence. Dad worked for a tailoring business and he was a foreman cutter. The whole company was evacuated to Weston-Super-Mare to make soldiers' uniforms. Our family moved to the seaside where we lived in a bungalow practically on the beach. Although only approaching three years old I had a friend who was a big girl, at least five; she would take me for walks. One day we crossed a field and were chased by cows! We ran as fast as a three year old and a five year old could. A kind lady who lived in a caravan took us in and gave us a drink of orange squash.

Sometime after this I was in Black Notley Hospital with T.B. I remember that quite well. I remember when 'they' moved us children from one ward to another. We were put into one of those large wicker laundry trolleys on wheels and pushed to a different part of the hospital.

BLACK NOTLEY

Through large glass windows
she watched all the people go by.
Lying there wondering, does she know
that when she gets here it will be time to say Goodbye.
The distant paths wind through the grounds,
the well-known figure goes walking past.
This way - I'm here. Don't go that way round.
We've moved. Let me go back. She walks so fast.
The figure recedes into the distance.
The glass holds back the screams and tears.
White clad nurses walk by without a second glance
as the child succumbs to all her fears.
This will be her place forever and a day,
no one will come to see her, or take her home.
On this iron bed, in this grey ward she'll stay
and no matter how long she cries, no one will come.

The ward had big opening windows so that we could get fresh air and our beds were pushed out whenever possible. There was a young girl, in a boat-shaped bed? She had TB in her spine and had to keep flat. I had my third birthday there. Mum had made a cake which she brought in. We children all sat at little tables down the middle of the ward for our tea and by the time it got to me my cake was all gone! My Dad was also in hospital, but I'm not sure which one; I think it was Chadwell Heath.

1941

I came home to Walthamstow from hospital to our home in Wetherdon Street. There was a little bike for me (Carole was on it. Mum said, "Let her ride, she's only little". So that is how it was!) I remember there was a huge pile of broken glass in the garden from the bomb damage upstairs, to the side of the house. I fell over and cut my hand; I still have the scar eighty years later. When Auntie Elsie and Derek and Margaret came back after being evacuated, we had to move out. Then we lived with Grandma and Grandad, Dad's parents, in Albany Road.

Going back over eighty years and thinking about our clothing, it is not only material itself that has changed, it is so many other things - washing facilities, central heating, man-made fibres, mass production, and last but not least cost.

1942/3
We moved to Durban Road. Carole and I often had to sleep under the table.

The day we moved Carole and I (aged 3 and 5) sat on the stairs with sandwiches for our lunch. This was obviously during 'the blitz' as it was called. When we first moved in, we often had to sleep under the table. As children we mostly slept but often woke up covered in soot from the chimney. One night we slept, but it was a close thing! Soot came down the chimney. Carole and I were smothered. Doodlebugs were dropping all around.

One night 'Craney' from next door but one (he was home on leave) was in the street in his pyjamas shouting, "They've hit the bleedin' gas works". (An aside! Just after Dad died Mr Crane popped into Mum's house, trying to chat her up!). One bomb had dropped in Billet Road right next to the school - three houses came down, four new ones were built. Then we got an air raid shelter in the garden. We slept in that during air raids.

Dad came home from one of his regular visits at the chest clinic to say I could finally go to school, 'Open Air School', Hale End Road. I was picked up by coach. Good. I remember one day we missed the coach, and I cried my eyes out. Mum made me some school blouses out of Dad's old shirts and when I had 'rough and tumbles' with the bigger boys coming home from school in the bus, the material tore quite easily. School was good. As you learnt you went up to another class, so I progressed. Also we all had a 'sleep' in the afternoons. One afternoon two bigger girls (8 or 9) had skipped out to buy sweets. When they got back Gladys (fair hair, legs in irons) and her friend were 'slippered'; she was very short and tubby with bright red knickers!!

1944

I went to Roger Ascham Junior School, Billet Road. They put me in the lowest class, then the teacher must have spoken to Head and I was moved up after one week into the 'A' class. In those days though, you had to stay in the same age group, you were not allowed to go into a higher group. My sister Carole went to the Infants, a separate building further down the road (actually so did my husband Frank's brother Don, who was also born in 1940 - the same age, what a coincidence). I enjoyed school. We went home for lunch between 12 – 1.30 then finished in the afternoon at 3.45.

1945

War ended. Mum made me a fairy dress out of crepe paper for the fancy dress party at school. I went to a works party with Mr & Mrs Maryson, our next-door neighbours, which was held in a hall near the Crooked Billet. His firm gave a party for all the children at a community centre near The Billet which we, Carole and I, went to. Their girls were a lot older; Jean was a nurse and Bernice slightly younger, finishing school, probably 14.

Another thing around this time was the man who used to come round with a horse and cart with a roundabout and collect all the empties and we would get a ride.

Obviously we would have to beg Mum for the bottles and jars because she would need them herself for making jams and pickles.

Because where we lived was a cul-de-sac we could play rounders, leap-frog, hide and seek either in the street or out the back in the field.

1946

That Easter was very nice weather-wise. Mum made Carole and me matching skirts. mine was a nice silver grey and Carole's was red. They were pleated and had shoulder straps with embroidery on. I think she also crocheted some gloves for us. We had an outing on the top of the bus to St Albans where we had been evacuated for a while. The people were nice and pleased to see us but I did not really remember them. Coming home on the bus, Mum sat with her new brown handbag that Dad had bought for her on her lap for the journey, and it melted in the sun. It was made of the new 'plastic' material!

When food, in its broadest sense, became part of my general knowledge, one of my earliest memories is shopping with Mum. Sainsbury's was a must. There were no supermarkets then but Sainsbury's was a shop that did all dairy produce. It was a long narrow shop with several serving areas, I would say about six possibly. Butter and margarine, then cheese and bacon, eggs, corned beef goes in there somewhere to be sliced, then some tinned goods and jars with jam. I can't remember how it was divided. I know we used to queue at each till.

Most things were rationed, the cheese for example was allowed at so many ounces per person, with ration books to be passed over the counter to the assistant. There were often 'make-pieces' on the cheese, little bits on top of the big piece where the assistant had not cut quite enough with their wire cutters. When we got out of the shop, if Mum was in a good mood, I would get the ounce of cheese to nibble.

Sweets were rationed as well. When we got a bit older, I think about eight or nine, my sister and I were given our sweet coupons with our one shilling and sixpence pocket money to go to the shop and get what we wanted. I saved mine up for a couple of weeks and got a quarter pound box of chocolates! That was about half a dozen individual sweets in a box. Carole used to get lots of penny things, chews and sherbet dabs.

1947

We were lucky in that although we were in Greater London, we had some fields and lanes at the back of us. That was the memorable winter with lots of snow and little coal available. Across a field and down a lane there was the gypsy encampment. Carole and I (aged 7 and 10) had to go there with a sack and half-a-crown to get logs from the encampment. They had geese wandering around and half a dozen old caravans; their horses were kept in the field. The gypsies were friendly but we were more concerned with the geese wandering around.

1948

I failed the eleven plus. I went to Chapel End School by trolley bus to the Billet then back again in the evening. These were our only means of transport. There were diesel buses at the Billet but you needed a trolley bus to get there. (There was a pub called The Crooked Billet; the traffic junction took its common name from that). I also used the trolley buses for going to Girl Guides in the evening. The trolley buses had 'arms' that connected to electric wires so they could not overtake each other. At busy times such as school leavings or factory or office closures there would be two or three coming along, having caught up. If they were full, they would allow five people standing, inside only.

One evening when it was dark (I was probably about eleven) I got off the bus and started walking up the road. I saw a gang of older kids tormenting someone, calling names, pushing and shoving, then they all ran away and he was left bewildered, probably lost. Then he headed across the road in my direction. I shouted at him, "You can't frighten me", and ran like mad! I got home but did not say anything. Mum asked me "Are you all right?". She gave me some bread and jam then I went to bed. Next day one of the other kids asked Mum how I was after the eventful evening.

Apparently, she found out, the youth I had seen was known locally. He came from a large family a few streets away and lived in a hospital. Today we would say he was intellectually disabled. When he was visiting his home he was looked after by his elder brothers. Years later I got to know him well.

1949
I enjoyed Senior School. Our teacher was Mr Fox. He kept control; even the noisier or naughtiest boys would obey Mr Fox. He ran a fencing group after school for the boys. It was just for boys! The classroom had a sloping floor and we sat in alphabetical order.

Sweets were still rationed although ice lollies came into fashion. We did not have television in those days so entertainment was from the radio. 'Dick Barton' would clear the field behind our house at 6.45 every evening.

1950
For a laugh some of us requested to sit for the thirteen plus examination. Lo and behold, I passed. I'm not sure

who was more surprised, me or the school. So that was another change, from Secondary Modern to Technical School. My youngest sister, Heather, was born 26.9.1950. I stayed at Auntie Mabel & Uncle Ralph's. Carole stayed with Uncle Fred and Auntie Elsie, Derek and Margaret.

1951

In September I went to South West Essex Technical School. It was in three parts. I went to Winns Avenue, the first part, which was an old Primary School building that had been converted. It was different to the Secondary School. We had a very nice teacher, a big motherly lady. Then there was a big old house in Hoe Street which was two buses away, with outbuildings converted to a Science block. The third part was next to the Town Hall in Forest Road.

King George died. A special school assembly was called. We all had to go to the third building, the main school, where there was an announcement. There were lots of tears and then we were allowed home early.

1952

We had biology in one of the converted buildings. It had a really old mulberry tree outside, a beautiful tree. Apparently the leaves were used to feed silkworms.

At this school, boys and girls were allowed to play together. We played 'Kingy' or 'British Bulldog', where a ball was thrown at people's legs. The game started with one person throwing the ball and every time they hit someone that person joined with the original player until all players were after the last one.

Physics was my favourite subject and chemistry was OK. I enjoyed English and maths.

Also this was the year of the famous London SMOG' (December 5- 9). It was so bad one couldn't see a hand in front of one's face. Dad had to walk home from work because there were no buses. He worked in Hackney. It took a couple of hours for him to walk home. Many people died from this thick fog. It did however start the clean-air programme. Smokeless fuel was promoted and bonfires banned.

1954

Dad was poorly again so I left school a year early in July, at the end of that school year. Mother came up to the school and asked; "Will she pass these (GCE) exams?" The school replied obviously, "We couldn't possibly say". Mum retorted, "Well she can leave and go out to work then!". I was supposed to be a nursery nurse but not with a history of TB. So Mum and I went for an interview at the Labour Exchange who sent us to Solmedia Laboratory Suppliers. Mum came with me! They were quite strict Plymouth Brethren, and I got the job! Why? Because I had good marks and comments for Religious Instruction! Never mind the good science marks. I started work with them in August.

Maureen   *1939 to 1958*

I was born 10 days before the outbreak of war, though in a 'safe' part of the country. My father, who as a plumber was in a reserved occupation, joined the Home Guard. My mother was a housewife, a full-time occupation in those days. Money was tight but thanks to rationing and thrifty parents we had all we needed.

My mother always described herself as a good plain cook. She had just come through the 'Hungry Thirties' so the privations of wartime were nothing new to her. She knew how to manage on very little. In fact, rationing meant that everyone had a chance of a balanced diet, so I never remember her complaining.

The cheapest cuts of meat were what she was used to cooking and these were generally available, affordable, tasty and nutritious. Bacon could be relied upon to make a tasty dinner. Liver was very healthy, though I disliked it. Kippers were too bony for me. Fortunately we never had to eat tripe. There were specialist tripe shops in the town and it was very cheap but my mother hated it and spared us ever having to find out what it was like.

Eggs were a problem for someone who did all her own baking. She refused on moral grounds to buy black market eggs, so she had to make do with powered egg or use recipes that did not need eggs. We had never heard of scrambled eggs, so we did not miss those. Omelettes were 'foreign' and not good for English stomachs. Boiled eggs were not possible. The only option was fried eggs, made by mixing powdered egg with water. We children, knowing nothing else, loved them.

Cheese came in very hard dry blocks. It was often described as 'soapy' and was known as 'mousetrap'. The fact that adults found it unsatisfactory did not stop us eating it.

One meal that we often had was called 'onion scones'. A slice of onion was sandwiched between two slices of potato then dipped in a batter made from flour, water, salt, pepper and a touch of vinegar, and deep fried in a pan of hot dripping. From the cheapness of the ingredients, I now assume this recipe was a legacy from those same 'Hungry Thirties'.

Adults drank tea; children drank mostly water. My mother did not approve of fizzy drinks, which we called 'pop'. We loved to drink Welfare orange juice, which was obtainable for free, courtesy of the government. It came highly concentrated in small bottles, one per child per week, only available at the 'Welfare', a weekly meeting of mothers and nursing staff that kept an eye on the general well-being of the children.

The sweet ration that was such a trial to some was no such thing to our family. We always had spare coupons because we rarely bought sweets during my early years. We were allowed the occasional bag of sherbet dab or stick of liquorice root that we sucked until there was no taste left. Later, we had the occasional bar of Cadbury's Dairy Milk and later still a plain chocolate called Oliver Twist.

One treat was provided by the American Government for every child in the UK. It was a small triangular paper bag containing a mixture of cocoa and sugar. We dipped our fingers in the bag then licked them. It tasted like nothing we had ever had before! Sometimes we badgered our parents to mix some up for us. We considered ourselves very fortunate if they gave in.

Everything I wore was identical to my sister's. For most of the year I wore a vest, liberty bodice, knickers (home-made in printed cotton with elastic waist and legs), blouse & skirt, cardigan and knee-high socks (grey or beige) with shoes or clogs. In Summer it was white ankle socks & sandals. The liberty bodice was like a corset but without the bones, long enough to tuck inside the knickers. It was made from an interlock cotton fabric and had built-up shoulders and small cotton covered buttons. I always had a coat and bonnet which were home-made; they had to last 2 years.

For gloves I remember wearing Dad's socks in 1947. My first pair of proper gloves was astrakhan-backed and came from Father Christmas. My grandma once gave me some hand-knitted fair isle mittens for Christmas. After my sister had been taught at school, we always knitted our own mittens – and I still work to the same pattern today.

Summer dresses were home-made usually in printed cotton. In 1946 we had 'French dresses' in a green floral print, with a placket at the neck fastened with poppers instead of the usual buttons down the front. For our grandparents' golden wedding my mother made us dresses in artificial silk with smocking on the puff sleeves, across the chest and all round the waist – an extraordinary amount of work.

During the 1940s there were very few vaccines. My sister and I were inoculated against diphtheria but nothing else. We had the usual childish ailments – chicken pox and measles. Many of our contemporaries got mumps but we escaped both that and German measles.

I suffered from repeated bad colds which always led to ear infections. These were very painful and lasted a long time as they could only be treated with warm olive oil in the ear since penicillin was not yet available. When I was three it was decided that I should have my tonsils removed in the hope that this would alleviate the problem. I remember being taken to the nearby hospital on the bus, my gas mask slung across my shoulders. There was no provision for parents to stay with their children, so I was alone for the first time in my life.

Another girl told me excitedly that she was looking forward to the operation because we would be given jelly and ice cream afterwards. I had never had ice cream and I am not sure I even knew what it was.

I was undressed and put into a bed, and it wasn't even bedtime. Then a nurse came to give me a big tablet to swallow. I refused. I told her I couldn't do it because I couldn't even swallow a Little Liver Pill. I cried, a lot. I kept pushing away the glass of water and inevitably spilled it down my nightdress. That annoyed the nurse because she then had to find some dry clothes to change me into. Eventually she managed to force the tablet down my throat and I remembered nothing more. For years I was convinced that it was the tablet that had removed my tonsils.

Back home the next day I was fed liquid foods – certainly not ice cream and I don't remember any jelly either!

When I was seven my sister got scarlet fever. The doctor wanted her to go to hospital but she cried and pleaded to be allowed to stay at home. She was put to bed in my parent's room where there was a fireplace. A sheet soaked in disinfectant was hung over the door.

I knew nothing of this at the time because I was packed off to go and live with my grandmother for six weeks to avoid my catching it. She lived only a mile or so away in a two up, two down weaver's house with a wash basin in the main bedroom and a toilet at the end of the yard. A very steep staircase ran up between the rooms. The 'parlour', as she always called it, was only ever used on special occasions so always smelt musty.

My sister and I were very close so life felt very strange without her and my parents. It felt equally strange when we were eventually reunited at the end of the six weeks.

The only way that ordinary working folk could pay the doctor's bills was by instalments. As a child I remember the 'doctor's man' calling every Friday evening for his half-crown (twelve and a half pence) to pay for our normal childish ailments. People often refused to see a doctor for fear of what it might cost, so treatable conditions went untreated. Family members took years to pay off the debts incurred during a deceased relative's final illness. All this changed when the National Health Service began and health care became free for everyone at the point of need, a principle that is still proudly maintained in spite of everything.

I adored my older sister and copied her in everything. I was longing to join her at school and started just before the end of the war.

The Primary School was about a mile from home, so we usually went by bus (tickets were free), though we walked in fine weather. Classes were large, as many as fifty-four one year. Discipline was strict and corporal punishment was accepted for older children.

Everyone started school the term before their 5th birthday. My first year at school was still in wartime. There was an air-raid shelter just outside the school gate, though

I only remember ever having one practice session. There were no seats in the shelter, so each child had to bring a cushion from home on their first day, after which it stayed at school. My mother had made mine from leftover material, with a carrying handle on the back.

The Infants' School had its own building and playground but was on the same site as the Junior School. It was in a good working-class area of town and it had a very good reputation. The headmistress of the Infants was a tall buxom lady, very forbidding to a five-year-old, though we discovered that she was very friendly and kindly. She taught sewing to small groups of final year girls in her own study, a small but light and cosy room. We did a lot of talking and quite a bit of giggling as well as sewing, but she did not seem to mind.

Every week each class would have a Band lesson, with simple instruments – triangles, black castanets on sticks, tambourines (there were only a few of these) and drums (even fewer). Cloth sheets printed with music were hung over a blackboard at the front of the room, each instrument on a different line and in a different colour. I was nearly always given a triangle (blue) but I longed to play something more rare, especially a drum. I suspect the teachers spotted my lack of musical ability and deliberately hid me amongst the numerous triangles! Once a year, on Empire Day, the whole school marched around the playground to the music of the Band as we waved our Union Jacks.

Another annual event was the sports day, held in the school yard. One race I particularly remember I was running so fast that I could not stop at the finishing line and ran smack into the brick wall of the outdoor shelter; my nose felt flat for days!

Playtimes were outdoors in all but the most exceptional weather. We played all the usual games plus a few that arose from our wartime childhoods. Aeroplanes were not very common in the skies over Burnley but when one flew overhead some children would jump up and down shouting: "My Daddy's up there! My Daddy's up there!" One day I joined in and was severely told off by one of the others. She said "You can't say that! Your Daddy hasn't gone away, your Daddy's at home!" I was very crestfallen; I thought it was just a game and had no idea that it really meant something to them.

During my first year in the Juniors we had a very exotic new arrival in our class, though she did not stay long. She was called Margaret McDonald and she was a dancer with the Flying Ballet that was appearing at the Victoria Theatre. I named my doll after her.

There was a boy called Albert who had been kept down because he struggled with every subject; all the rest of us could read better than he could, even though he was a year older. With the casual cruelty of children, we called him a dunce.

At that time, the whole country was being encouraged to save, children being no exception. Those who could afford it took a few pence to school each week and had the sum recorded in a deep blue bank book. When we had accumulated a pound, the money was transferred to a paler blue book which we had to bring from home. The money I saved went on our annual summer holiday.

The teacher in the next to top class kept discipline with a strap across the palm of the hand. More than once I had to go home and confess that I had had the strap for talking in class. I got no sympathy, just "Well you must have deserved it". My writing did not come up to his exacting standards and I, along with several others, was given a book of proverbs which we had to copy using precisely ruled lines; I do not think I ever mastered that to his satisfaction.

The top-class teacher used a cane, though less frequently because most of us had been licked into shape by that time. She was keen on nature and would identify any flowers we took into school using a little reference book. Many of the flower names I know today came from her. She had also travelled, at a time when few people did. She had been to Australia and described how the grass was scorched brown in summer, something unheard of on the slopes of the Pennines! She had also been to Canada and told us about the great lakes and the huge snowfalls that were even greater than we had in the cold winter of 1947.

The desks were set out in rows, with boys on the left and girls on the right, arranged in exam results order, starting with the brightest at the back corner. Exams, or Tests, came twice a year at Christmas and Summer. In our final year we had the 11+ Exams in the Spring. We were thoroughly prepared for them, though without the intense pressure of today's Stats. I ran all the way home when we got the results and my mother took me straight into town to buy my new uniform. Some children were promised new bicycles if they passed; I was not promised anything, but my sister and I were bought our first watches as a reward.

After school and during the holidays we 'played out' – that is, we met up with other boys and girls from the estate and played games in the cinder-surfaced street. Some older children had bicycles; I shared one with my sister, which meant that I hardly ever rode it. We built dens in the fields and in the winter of 1947 we built them in a six-foot snowdrift.

Radio was important, both Children's Hour and the more grown-up 'Dick Barton, Special Agent'. A cry of "Time for Dick Barton" cleared the street instantly at 6:45!

My sister and I went to Sunday School from the time I was three years old. If our attendance was good enough we were given a prize, a voucher to spend at the book shop in town. As we grew older we took part in concerts on the stage in the upstairs school room. Later still we joined the choir in staging rough and ready performances of musicals.

When I was thirteen my brother was born, which changed everything for me. Home life became centred around this new arrival with ginger hair whom we adored.

Out of school we began to have shop-bought clothes when I was about 13 though at first everything still matched my sister's. From about 15 we were allowed to be fashionable. From that time we had an annual trip to Manchester on the bus to buy a winter coat for best wear. Hats came from local shops. My first high heels were brown Cuban-heeled court shoes by K.

At 17 I had a mid-calf grey pencil skirt (home-made) worn with pink nylon lace blouse with cap sleeves. That summer A-line dresses were in fashion; ours were in blue & white cotton with a square neck, no sleeves and a 3-tiered skirt. The next year it was a dress in seersucker with a circular skirt and cap sleeves.

At about 18 I was bought a light woollen summer suit in a butter & white tiny check. I was made to wear a girdle to keep my tummy in! It was supposed to be light control, but I hated the constriction. With the suit was matched a pale blue nylon blouse with an embroidered edge to the collar, cream court shoes with higher heels, nylon stockings with seams, nylon lace gloves and a white plastic bag.

Burnley Girls' High School began in 1910, temporarily housed on two floors of the Technical College. It was still there when I entered the First Form in 1951! The two establishments were strictly separated. No girl was to look at a College student, even if he was her own brother, a law that was enforced by mandatory Order Mark (the loss of one mark from your House's total for the term). There was a great sense of anticipation when the first turf was cut for a new building on a large site on the border between Burnley and Padiham, some two miles from the centre of town.

At first most children went home for lunch, only the unlucky few with working mothers stayed for school dinners. This changed when the High School moved into the new building. There was a large dining room that could accommodate all the girls in sittings.

The food we were served was very similar to what we would have had at home, stews, meat pies and fish on a Friday for the sake of the Roman Catholics, though there were very few of those in Burnley. Being a fussy eater, I did not like either cheese or onions, so cheese and onion pie was a disaster for me. I only went hungry a few times before learning to put up with it.

We all liked the baked puddings with custard which we had three or four times a week. Sago was not a favourite with anyone, but I did not mind it as I was used to milk puddings. One day the school was permeated by a terrible smell from mid-morning onwards. We were finally told that the cooks were experimenting with a synthetic meringue and that it tasted much better than it smelled, quite good in fact. Not everyone was brave enough to try it.

Uniform was strict – brown gym slip (regulation length unfashionably short), tussore blouse, tie and cardigan, brown coat, beret and shoes. Summer uniform (brown and white gingham dress) was introduced in my fourth year. In the Sixth Form we were allowed to wear skirts instead of gym slips, still brown, though.

There were ninety girls in each Year, divided into three Forms of thirty. These were labelled A, B and C and were allocated according to overall ability. Occasionally a girl would be moved up or down, but the vast majority stayed in the same stream all the way up to the Fifth Form.

Mostly we studied the same subjects, though Form A spent less time on the practical subjects, only two years of Sewing and later one of Cookery in the Fifth Form (if you did not choose the Extra Science option to prepare for taking Science subjects in the Sixth Form). The other big difference came in the Second Year, when the A Form began Latin, the B Form began German, and the C Form did not take an extra language. Everyone took French, and all subjects except Art were taken up to the fifth year, making nine GCE subjects plus Scripture and Games/Gym/PT.

We were not allowed to talk during lessons; punishment was an Order Mark, which I earned more than once. A more major misdemeanour was eating in class, punished by a Detention. That meant one day in the next week staying for half an hour after school writing out lines. The worst form of punishment was a Conduct Mark; three of these in a year meant expulsion. No girl had ever earned three Conduct Marks In her whole time at the school until our year. One girl was particularly badly behaved and defiant of everyone, including the Headmistress. There was much talk of her being expelled but she never was, though there was general relief when she left as soon as she could, at the end of the Fourth Form.

Unfortunately for me Gym was one of the end-of-year exams. We spent many lessons sitting with our faces to the wall as girls were called individually to perform their exercise. Talking was forbidden, the penalty being to lose five marks. Arranged in alphabetical order we knew when we would be called so anxiety grew as our turn came nearer. There was one very curious element to the marking system for the Gym exams. School rules dictated that our gym slips should be at least five inches above the knee when kneeling. During the exam we had the length of our gym slips measured. If it was less than five inches above your knee, you lost ten marks! Anyone who got 70% or over got a gym badge, a small strip of green ribbon to wear on the gym slip.

The Borough Council's Education Committee was very keen that working class children should have their horizons expanded. One result was that every two years a private train was hired to take pupils from all of the Secondary Schools in the town to a place that was normally inaccessible to us. Each school had its own designated carriages, mixing being deemed undesirable.

The first expedition was to the Festival of Britain in London (1951), a trip of over 24 hours without sleep! The next one was to Edinburgh. The train left at five in the morning so we had to get up at three in order to have breakfast and get to the station in time. We travelled over the Forth Bridge (the old one!) and then back on the ferry to visit the castle. In the afternoon we went to the zoo, a first for most of us. My sister was so excited and tired after the trip that she told our parents the elephants were pink!

Subsequent trips took us to York (a museum with a street in it!) and Oxford (a sail on the river then a tour of a college).

Every year our school had a trip abroad for girls from the fourth year upwards (15+). Foreign travel was very expensive so numbers were quite small. Our parents somehow found the money for my sister to go to Paris in the first year sixth form and for me to go to Bruges when I reached the same stage. I can still remember the excitement as the train left Burnley station.

In 1952 King George VI died. The next day the whole school was assembled in the main hall, sitting cross-legged on the floor as usual, to listen to the proclamation of the new Queen. Someone had managed to rig up a radio and speakers for the broadcast. Our astonishment that this could be done made the occasion memorable.

To celebrate the Coronation the Secondary Schools of the town put on a pageant of queens of England on the outdoor stage in Towneley Park. Our school chose Matilda - no one else wanted her as so little was known about her reign. The senior history teacher wrote a script in verse. The art teacher designed all the costumes and used older girls to make helmets from cut-down hats painted silver; wooden swords were made, and daggers and shields from scrap metal sourced from goodness knows where. Everyone who could knit was conscripted into making armour out of dishcloth cotton subsequently painted silver. We had a fabulous time on stage fighting with wooden daggers, swords and battle axes. One person in the audience was heard to remark on what a good time those boys down there were having! We were, of course, all girls.

I joined the school Girl Guide troop, though never went to camp.

One year I took part in the school play as a professor of philosophy in 'Le Bourgeois Gentilhomme' (type-cast, many thought).

At church I graduated into the Youth Forum, a valuable training ground for thinking Christians. I also joined the choir, though I was not a good singer. I still remember some of the pieces we sang, in particular The Hallelujah Chorus.

Jude   *1944 to 1961*

1944

I was born in January 1944 at Wymering, Portsmouth, during an air raid. I lived with my mother's mother (Baba Hamilton) in Cosham until 1947.

1947

It was the most bitterly cold winter on record with thick snow everywhere. Baba took me by bus and train to Nyetimber, a village just west of Bognor Regis in West Sussex to meet 'Mummy and Daddy', the latter having recently returned from India where he had been stationed during the war. I screamed non-stop for days at her leaving me with these unknown people.

I went to school straight away – a special dispensation – not only because my mother was seriously ill with T.B. but also because I was able to read and write and add up and had learned a few times tables off by heart. At the age of three I was put into a class of five year olds and hauled out from the back of the class to read things, then, when 5, up to the Junior School where they put me into a class of seven year olds. I sat at the back with my own work to do. I was not allowed out to the playground after the other children tried, and almost succeeded, in strangling me with a skipping rope. I was considered by the other children as a bit of a freak and kept apart as if a leper on account of my mother having died of T.B. I was probably a precocious little brat anyway.

1948

This year saw the installation of central heating in my parents' house. The house was at the end of a fairly long drive, with a garage and outbuildings where the radiators were stored in a neat row, except that one was out of line. I tried to straighten it but it fell on top of me and I was pinned underneath for what seemed like hours before they found me. I have a recollection of my legs being in callipers for some time afterwards. The four huge radiators were installed downstairs only. They were heated from a large coal fired stove in the kitchen which for some reason did not heat the water. This was heated by an immersion heater in a cupboard just outside my bedroom.

The coal merchant delivered coal to the bunkers built at the back of the garage. I used to watch these grimy-faced huge men carry hessian sacks of coal on their backs and tip the contents into the bunkers. One summer aged about 5 I had thoroughly cleaned one of the bunkers to use as a den using a scrubbing brush and plenty of soap and water and was horrified when one of these burly men tipped the contents of his sack all over my treasures inside it.

The French onion man came every summer, his bike festooned with onions and wearing a Breton beret. He would sing French songs as he pedalled along the lane at the bottom of our drive and would whistle to let everyone know he was there.

The knife grinder also came regularly with his honing wheel strapped to his handlebars and turned by his pedals. I was fascinated by the sparks it threw off.

Pheasants, hares, rabbits and ducks, all still with feathers and fur, were delivered and were hung from hooks from the rafters in the 'game room' (another outbuilding at the rear of the garage) until they were 'high' enough.

The fishmonger called with his horse and cart full of fresh fish caught that morning. The milkman came every morning and left pint bottles of unpasteurised milk which were left at the end of the drive.

No-one had a refrigerator then until the fifties. There was a larder with a stone shelf and an air brick to keep things cool. Sometimes the milk went sour and was strained through muslin cloths and made into cottage cheese.

Most people, if they had a garden, had chickens, and we were no exception. I remember being in a party dress and trying to find a chicken feeding bowl my mother had mislaid and scrambling up to the top of the chicken coop to retrieve it. Instead of being pleased my mother was horrified at the state of my party dress, which was torn, dirty and unwearable. I did not go to the party.

1950

My mother died aged 34 on Christmas day. As an army officer (Queen Alexandra Nursing Corps) she had been in the King Edward V11 sanatorium in Midhurst for a long time. I can remember, before she died, and on one of the few times she was at home, standing holding her hand waiting for a bus. She explained to me what a passing hearse was and that soon she would be carried away in one of them, but I was not to be afraid and must always be strong. On another occasion I remember sitting with her in the field next to our house which was a wonderful meadow the like of which one does not see these days. It was full of blue cornflowers, red poppies, multicoloured lupins and other flowers. It was a riot of colour. She asked me if I knew what happened to the colour of the flowers after they died. She told me that God would put all the colours into the rainbow, and that when she died God would put the colour of her into the rainbow as well, so that when I saw one I would know she was up there keeping an eye on me and sending her love down the sunbeams. She prepared me so well for her death that I did not really miss her when she was gone. She had been in hospital on and off for as long as I had known her and any close bond had probably been broken anyway.

1951

After my mother died, I ran wild. I was out all day in all weathers, and often nights as well while my father was away. He used to go away a lot, leaving me entirely on my own. As a hobby, and being an accomplished pianist, he had formed his own jazz/dance band which was much in demand, so he played away a lot county-wide. As soon as he left I would get up from bed and roam the countryside in the dark (even on the wildest stormy nights) with the hooting of owls, the sound of the Owers lightship and the barking of foxes for company. I recognised the sound of his car from miles away and as soon as I heard that distinctive engine noise, I would race back from wherever I was to get back into bed before he came home. My feet (always bare) knew every inch of the ground by feel alone Sometimes my father did not return that night at all.

My father fed me on books and fiendishly hot Madras curries but frequently forgot to leave any food when he was away, so at times I would scrump stuff from neighbouring orchards and other people's kitchens when they were out. I became an accomplished burglar, able to shin up drainpipes, climb roofs and squeeze through half open skylights.

I remember one occasion finding a very pink, cooked lobster sitting on a plate on a kitchen table, which proved an irresistible temptation to a hungry child. With utmost difficulty, and by standing precariously on kitchen shelves and the top of a large fridge, I managed to get myself and the lobster back through the half open skylight through which I had entered. Once out, I stuffed the lobster under my jumper and raced home where I smashed it to bits with stones and a hammer and using an awl and a screwdriver. I ate the lot in one go. It was delicious. I buried the remains in a faraway ditch. Because it was an affluent neighbourhood, I was actually quite well fed on the choicest of foodstuffs and despite rationing still being in force.

As I have said, I mostly went bare foot, truly feral. I was able to run over pebbles on the beach with no shoes with ease, and also to climb trees and run over fields of thistles and nettles without getting stung. I knew instinctively how to avoid such obstacles. I vaulted five-bar gates, negotiated tiny gaps in thorny hedgerows, navigated ditches and streams, made dens out of branches and twigs always of course on my own. I do not recall having any friends but I did have a very real imaginary family with whom I had audible conversations.

Not knowing anything different, I was not unhappy. Indeed I think I was extremely happy. I was utterly free. No-one called me in for meals or bedtimes. I could do what I liked, when I liked and how I liked. If I wanted to travel ten or so miles across fields, exploring all day, there was no-one to stop me. Sometimes I would borrow a neighbour's dog. Bruno the alsatian and Whiskey the fox terrier became firm friends.

I used to have long blonde plaits which were done for me by the cleaning lady, Mrs Wyatt who came daily, early in the morning. But she changed her hours, so my father took me to his barber in the village and ordered him to give me a 'short back and sides'. I was devastated and ashamed at the loss of my hair and to this day dread going to the hairdressers, (I would much prefer the dentist) or having my hair cut above the ear line.

1952

I was eight and caught chicken pox, necessitating a sort of isolation for a few weeks but that did not bother me in the slightest. It only meant not going to school.

I remember coming second in maths at school and my father telling me that no child of his ever came second in anything and shut me in my bedroom for the weekend to study the particular topic I had failed in. He left a jug of water and cold porridge outside my bedroom door.

King George VI died. I remember at school we were shown photographs from the newspapers of Princess (now Queen) Elizabeth on the steps of an aeroplane in East Africa about to fly home.

1953

This was the year that Stalin died. I remember being at my father's mother's house and the newspapers being full of the news. Uncle Joe (more about him later) gave me a history lesson, starting with the Russian Revolution and then how Stalin came to power and all about his atrocities. We were sitting in my grandmother's conservatory with sheaves of fresh tobacco hanging from the rafters to dry. Uncle Joe grew his own tobacco. I think that may have been illegal, but the smell of drying tobacco is something I have not forgotten.

This was the year I learned the facts of life from Brown Owl.

This was the year too when Baba Hamilton died. My father woke me up in the middle of the night to tell me that not only would I never see her again, but also that he was severing all links with that side of my family, and I would no longer be having any contact with my maternal aunts or cousins either. I never discovered why, but recall being very upset at the time. I had lived for my first three years with Baba and was fond of my cousins.

1954

My father had a few years previously started the habit in the early mornings of shouting, across the landing from his bedroom to mine, anagrams, word puzzles and mental arithmetic problems. I also had to review books he had given me to read. This two-way shouting across the landing continued for several years. I had to do all the puzzles entirely in my head and to ad lib the book reviews - no pencil or paper allowed.

I rode my bike and other people's horses, collected grass snakes, slow worms, hedgehogs and beetles which I kept under my bed until the cleaning lady (Mrs Wyatt) said she would come no more unless they were all removed. I relocated them to a large old doll's house behind the garage which had been taken out of the house because it was infested with woodworm, but not soon enough. She left anyway, for which event I was blamed, although years later I learned that she was fed up with my father too frequently forgetting to pay her.

I also collected stamps and picture postcards – both of which I still have. My fossil collection from hours and hours of neck-aching beachcombing was thrown away by my father during one of his rages at me.

I went to Brownies, and Sunday School twice each Sunday - in order, according to my father, to acquire moral fibre, in which he told me, I was singularly lacking. I did answer back a lot and always had to have the last word. I think now that he must have been at his wits' end as to how to cope with me. We had almighty arguments which usually ended by my lying on the floor, hyperventilating, suffering chronic nosebleeds and screaming non-stop until he poured a bucket of cold water over me.

I ran away this year, aged ten, and lived for several days in an old, abandoned caravan I had discovered miles out in the countryside, only coming out at night when it was dark. This caused a local search. My father was of course very angry but more concerned I think with the damage done to his local reputation. He was a pillar of the community. Chairman of the local Round Table, President of the local Motor Club, Steward at Goodwood Motor Racing Circuit amongst many other offices he held.

I came top of the county for the Eleven Plus and won several scholarships but my father, an ardent Socialist, refused to let me take any of them up. I never knew why he was a Socialist. It may have been an act of rebellion in his youth and he stuck with it. I do not recall him being up in arms over worker's rights or on the side of the underprivileged. Certainly he was concerned that I did not become 'overprivileged' - hence the reason for insisting I was educated via the state system. His mother was a Conservative.

My father's mother insisted I had piano lessons and paid for them, so I practised and practised obsessively, which drove my father mad when he was at home - to such an extent he took to locking the piano, but I discovered where he had hidden the key so practised when he was out or away. She was a Yorkshire woman through and through, the daughter of a foundry owner, tough as old boots, a keen gardener, knitter, quilter, cook, whist and bridge player and the giver of my weekly bath.

My father was her only child. Her husband, his father, had been killed in WW1 and in WW2 her house was bombed by a doodlebug and looted. She was fond of saying "They took my husband in the first and my house in the second".

She never remarried but had always had admirers, notably 'Uncle Joe', who had apparently just turned up on her doorstep in Bognor one day and never left. He slept in one of her 'small bedrooms' and used to sit in her kitchen for hours at a time, on a wooden stool he had made, in meditation. He was the younger son of a younger son and somehow related to the Duke of Leeds. He certainly had the same family surname and owned most, if not all, of Armley in Leeds. He left his entire estate to my grandmother when he died in 1954.

My grandmother grew all her own fruit and vegetables I remember being sent out on frosty mornings to pick sprouts, and in the summer, gooseberries and blackcurrants which then had to be topped and tailed.

1955

At the next educational stage, aged 7, I had been put into a class of eleven year olds, where I languished at the back as usual. In the September I started at 'Chi High' (Chichester High School for Girls). There I met Jen, Jackie, Janie and Jilly – the five J's, a friendship that is still going strong today after all these years, although Jen died in 2007 so there are now only four of us.

I acted in school plays, always taking the 'character' parts such as a yokel, Richard (an orphaned clerk in Christopher Fry's 'The Lady's Not for Burning'), Miss Bates in Emma, and others. I also 'flew up' to Girl Guides.

Interestingly, this year, Rosemarie (another member of our writing group) started her teacher training course at Bishop Otter College in Chichester and pursued her hobby of campanology at the cathedral which was our school church. Without knowing it our paths had already crossed.

Our uniform at Chi Hi was bottle green, oatmeal, yellow and brown. We had Harris Tweed coats in winter with felt hats and woe betide us if we were caught without gloves. In summer we had blazers and straw boaters and again were not to be seen out of school without white gloves. Lower school wore tunics which had to be 'on the knee' but in Upper IV we could wear bottle green pleated skirts with straps. We wore brown sling purses and were taught to take pride in being well turned out. Jilly was always very neat and tidy but somehow I tended to look scruffy – a fact my father frequently remarked upon. I enjoyed school.

1956

My father remarried - a glamorous Kay Kendall look-alike fourteen years his junior and fourteen years my senior, and who brought with her a Morris Minor, a cocker spaniel called Junior, an air of sophistication and the pervasive smell of expensive perfume. I was pleased for him. We now had curtains at the windows, something my mother had never got round to doing. She tried her best to tame my wildness and to heal the growing rift between my father and myself.

This was the year of the Suez and Hungarian crises and the news was full of it. We now had a television. Most thought this was the start of WWIII. I recall being frightened.

This was the year also when Jackie and I were confirmed at Petertide by Bishop Bell of Chichester at St Thomas a Becket church in Pagham. I was devastated when the Bishop put his hands on me, that the Holy Spirit did not immediately descend upon me, looking anxiously up to the rafters for any sign of a dove – even a wood pigeon would have done.

Every Sunday thereafter, Jackie would cycle over from Runcton with her bathers and we would attend the 7.00am communion service at Pagham church, go for a swim then back to my house in Nyetimber for a jolly good breakfast cooked by my new stepmother.

1957

I was now 13 and starting my teenage years. Harold Macmillan became Prime Minister.

1958

My first half-sister was born and it was the year we discovered Elvis and 'rock and roll' and Church Guild dances. I also became a member of an extensive 'gang' locally. If one were not invited to at least three parties on a Saturday night one was not 'in' locally. All the parents knew each other and had parties of their own leaving us children to do as we liked. My parents were very social locally, as were all the other residents. They were friends with Cicely Courtneidge and Jack Hulbert who lived up the road in a house with iron gates the left hand one of which had the treble clef on it and the right one the bass clef. I had met Donald Campbell on several occasions; he frequently visited his relations over the road in the Aldwick Bay Estate (an exclusive private estate near Craigweil where King George V stayed and memorably said "Bugger Bognor") and Ginger Rogers and Fred Astaire had a holiday house not far from ours. Another local and well-known eccentric was the heir to J. Arthur Rank who maniacally rode his bicycle everywhere, talking to himself and trying to run over children who had the temerity to get in his way. It became a game of 'dare' if we saw him, to step into his path and watch him swerve and hopefully fall off his bike.

I learnt to drive fast cars on farms and private roads (two of the gang went on to become famous racing drivers). We had barbecues on the beach. We sailed, rode horses bareback at dawn on the sand when the tide was out, and enjoyed our teenage years. They were glorious innocent and wonderful days.

It was the year I got locked into Lincoln cathedral, only rescued by students at the next-door seminary getting hold of an enormous ladder so I could climb down it, through a window and escape into their forbidden grounds. That is another story for another time.

My stepmother organised a party for my 14th and gave me a Blue Persian kitten for a present. I called her Scheherazade. She was unfortunately deaf and one was able to drive a car up the drive almost on top of her lying outside the garage before she would move. She tried unsuccessfully to do the same with the local bus in the road at the end of the drive. I was utterly heartbroken at her untimely demise.

1959

O levels. I got distinctions in English Language, English Literature and British Constitutional History and, in retrospect, on quite wrong advice from my father opted for Biology, Chemistry and Zoology for A levels. Jen got 100% in Maths. Jackie did exceptionally well in German and Jilly in French. Our school was single-sex and we were forbidden to talk to any of the boys at Chi Hi for Boys, which anyway was not so long established as our school, which was still run on its previous lines of having once been part of the Girls' Public Day School Trust. Despite all this we all did well in our exams, O levels and then A levels. Between us we collected a lot of distinctions etc. We were considered a kind of 'intellectual elite', which we exploited to the full by being thoroughly misbehaved - running, for buttons, a thriving poker school; organising mock elections and getting the whole school out on to the playing fields instead of lessons one afternoon; replacing a framed butterfly collection with one of bluebottles and other nasty insects; handing in for homework satirical essays instead of what had been set and other naughty things.

1961

My great grandfather, aged 96, was living with my father's mother in Bognor, having left Filey a few years before, bringing with him his antique collection, his penny farthing bicycle and his own great grandfather's long case clock. He died in June of a broken heart when my grandmother chopped up the aforesaid clock in front of him.

My second half-sister was born in July. In September I came down for breakfast in my school uniform. "Go back upstairs and take that uniform off. You're not going back to school". In amazement, I managed to choke out "But what about Girton" (where I had secured a provisional place) before falling absolutely silent with severe aphasia for a period of about five weeks caused by the sheer shock of it.

Jocelyn   *1960 to 1978*

I was born in Cheltenham in 1960 where my mother was staying with her mother as my father, a naval officer, had to leave her during labour to re-join his ship. He first met me when I was about nine months old. We spent the next seven years living in married quarters and moving house every 2-3 years as Dad was posted either to different ships based at naval dockyards across England or to bases inland.

As a young child in the days before synthetic clothing or disposable nappies I remember best the feel of things. I was often in wool and have somehow acquired an aversion to 'scrunchy' plastic which I associate with plastic pants worn over nappies. Certainly, I remember helping my mother with the twin tub, and the washing line filled with my sisters' terry towelling nappies. One year they froze and were stiff as boards. Pictures show my sisters and me were always dressed very similarly, in wool jerseys with kilts or pinafores and woolly tights.

My first blazer was purchased at the age of four, for my first school, a nursery in Bath, required everyone to wear uniform. It was based in a Georgian terraced house where both boys and girls sat at individual, small wooden desks to draw, to repeat what had just been written on the blackboard and to read Janet and John books. There was also a shared ancient ceramic water closet from which we fled in fear after flushing because of the noises the cistern made.

We could wear our own clothes though at my next school, Solent Rd. The family had moved to Portsmouth where I graduated from the Infant to the Junior school. The photo accompanying this part of the book shows my class. We had won a painting competition with our pictures of HMS Victory following a school trip to the dockyard. It looks to me as if we were practising handwriting, Marion Richardson was then in vogue and we would spend hours copying out rows of loops and flourishes.

We were expected home for lunch every day. In the mid-1960s children walking short distances unsupervised was common. Food shopping was also done daily as household refrigeration was extremely rare and supermarkets had yet to reach towns outside London, though purchasing a joint of meat was a weekly affair. Meat was so important that in the larder there was a meat safe.

In fact, the week's meals centred around Sunday lunch which was always beef or lamb or maybe a roast chicken, that reappeared in various guises throughout the week. Cold meat with salad, offcuts in a stew or a goulash, or minced in a tomato sauce with rice – my mother was a great reader of cookery books and, between Elizabeth David and Constance Spry, food at home, well at least until Friday, was both tasty and nutritious. By Friday though the joint had been scraped to the bone and curried eggs were a very poor second choice. Cheesy potatoes (first baked in their skins then the contents mashed with butter and cheese before being grilled with bacon atop) were much preferred. The aforementioned bone though was never wasted. Boiled for hours and making the kitchen smell terrible in the process, it was the basis for next week's soup lunches with vegetables and pearl barley thrown in.

In Portsmouth we acquired a second-hand car, a black Morris Minor with indicators that flipped up from the side. We went on day trips to Hayling Island only for me and my two sisters to sit inside the car with packets of crisps (with the salt in its own little blue bag) and small bottles of lemonade for what seemed like hours while our parents spent the afternoon in a pub.

As a child I don't remember being unwell except for the indignity of being forced to inhale steam from a mixture of Friar's Balsam and hot water to clear a blocked nose. One year when I was 7 or 8, I am told I suffered badly from measles, spending weeks in a darkened room. Once back at Junior School though, I did well and regularly enjoyed coming top in the weekly tests. That is except when a young lad beat me to it; he was better at maths and we were vicious rivals.

Yet, when playtime came, boys and girls would gather separately. When our class teacher, Miss G, was on playground duty us girls would hang around with her to watch her smoke. Other times we organised our own games such as clapping rhymes or skipping ropes. More rarely boys and girls would mix freely when the shout went up for tag-based team games such as British Bulldog where the 'bulldogs' literally wrestled those caught to the ground, or, less painfully, Stick in the Mud. In the latter, if caught, you simply had to freeze in place with legs spread apart in case of potential rescue by an as-yet-uncaught member of your own team crawling through the gap.

After school we would walk between friends' houses to play. We lived towards the top of a hill where only a few families had cars and there was very little traffic to contend with. We played mostly outside except in the worst weather and there were regular parties, both birthday and fancy-dress, as our mothers got together to create entertainments while their men were at sea. The Aden crisis suddenly emptied the dockyard one year.

In 1968 we moved again when Dad was stationed in Singapore and where we spent an idyllic three years. Each married quarter came with its own staff, a cook amah, a wash amah and a garden boy who all took pride in looking after their 'family'. However, much of the subsequent wonderful Chinese and Malaysian cooking was wasted on me and my sisters who, instead, whined that the cornflakes were soggy, the milk disgusting and the eggs tasted of fish. Fortunately, Ah Yok tempted me to try her nasi goreng and today I actively travel to seek it out. Other highlights were satay at the Batik Inn, huge prawns caught that day at Kukup and all sorts of barbecued meats at the night markets which today are but a sanitised shadow of their past.

One of my greatest food memories dates from this time – a Primary School visit to an American Navy warship while it was docked. After the usual tour, we were taken to the galley and each child given a scoop of vanilla ice-cream and a cookie. My mouth waters to this day remembering the delicious shock of a buttery cookie and the rich, creamy taste of golden vanilla.

School was only ever in the morning and each afternoon we went swimming in the officers' pool. We would take snacks and drinks in Tupperware which made everything taste and smell of hot plastic.

Back in school uniform, a light cotton tunic, I was desperately uncomfortable, for the wash amah believed firmly in starching everything within in an inch of its life.

Subjects were the same as in the UK: maths, writing, science or nature and we worked towards taking the Eleven Plus. Despite everything being priced locally in dollars and cents we had to learn pounds, shillings and pence, which was generally felt to be horribly unfair as it was more difficult. Our project work centred around the local environment; examples included Malay dress and Malay industries. Our school visit to the Van Houten chocolate factory was the highlight of the year. We had weekly swimming lessons too, being made to miss swimming for doing poorly in spelling was a common punishment; others ranged from being made to stand up in class to being sent to see the Head.

I was a tomboy and regularly refused to wear dresses; my mother compromised and I went through several batik trouser suits. It was the late 60s, the Beatles were all the rage and our parents were wearing short Mary Quant style skirts (mothers) or brightly patterned shirts (fathers).

Banyans, picnics at sea, were the best. Fishing boats were hired and staffed with spare officers from the visiting ships. Equipped with a dustbinful of cans of beer for the adults and another one of Coca Cola for the kids we would cruise all day in the Straits, jumping in and swimming in crystal clear waters or aquaplaning – being towed on a board behind the boat.

There were dangers though. To this day, I will never touch a cone-shaped shell nor a jellyfish as we were regularly warned to stay well away as, in the tropics, stings could mean death before you could get treatment. Also it wasn't uncommon to see rabid dogs, though we were all very proud of our friend's dog, a small, tatty looking mongrel called Hector, who turned out not to be having a fit after all but alerting us to the presence of a spitting cobra.

I don't remember being given homework but know that we could complete our project folders at home, which I was keen to do. Again, there were regular events for children, spelling competitions and quizzes as well as Trafalgar Day and other naval celebrations.

On ordinary weekends though we would go round to the neighbours to watch their black and white television. We were particular fans of Dr Who and Bewitched. I was annoyed that we didn't get to watch the 1969 moon landing on television. At the time I wanted to be an astronaut and my father bought me a 45-rpm recording of Neil Armstrong's speech. We played it along with our other 45s such as 'Honey Honey', 'Lily the Pink' and, surreptitiously as it was banned by the right-wing government of Lee Kuan Yew, 'Puff the Magic Dragon' on a Bakelite gramophone.

Back in England in 1971 I never thought to question why I was sent to an all-girls private boarding school for my secondary education. There were quite a few other girls from naval families there, one or two of whom I had met before, so I expect the school was known to many.

It was a big shock. We were in a dormitory of ten with iron bedsteads, thin mattresses, blankets and candlewick bedspreads. The heating was a single pipe that ran round the room and, in winter, there was often ice on the inside of the windows. We used to undress carefully leaving our jerseys, shirts and ties slotted together so they could be thrown on, in one hurried go, in the cold mornings.

The food was unspeakable and we lived off the sticky buns provided at break along with sliced white bread and jam for tea. It was back to the British ideal that a meal should comprise meat and two veg, though as the slices of meat or ham invariably had a slick, sheen to them reflecting rainbow colours, the food was not in the least bit appetising. The vegetables were slightly better, boiled to a tasteless paste they could at least be swallowed without nausea. Mince, whether in cottage pie or an attempt at a watery bolognaise, was either grey or burned (or possibly dyed, I wouldn't put it past them) a brown-black. The net result was that nobody ate anything unless forced, which of course we were. Each table had a terrifying sixth-former in charge and your only option was to ask for a small portion, half of which could be hidden under your knife and fork. Consequently, we were all pasty and overweight which, with our school summer uniform of pink cotton dresses with blazers and hats, must have been an alarming sight in Westbourne each Saturday as we walked to the shops. We also had to attend church each Sunday, marching two by two, in long crocodiles and wearing white gloves as well as the hats.

Except for the regular power cuts, the national miners' strikes and three-day week, 1974 impinged little on our juvenile consciousness. The power cuts were resented as our 'dorm' was required to stay with the housemistress in her room and play interminable games of Beetle Drive when the electricity was out in the evenings.

The school itself, founded nearly one hundred years ago by two Victorian spinsters, could be pre-war in its outlook. We were indeed regularly told that 'us gals' were the 'crème de la crème' and I remember both ballroom dancing and deportment lessons amongst the main academic thrust. On Wednesdays and Saturdays team games were compulsory. I played goal in hockey (the only player allowed to wear tracksuit trousers) but preferred cricket and the accompanying team teas.

Once past puberty the temptation to rebel was irresistible but I was not sufficiently daring to be one of those girls who broke bounds to meet up with, even sleep with (if their tall tales were indeed true), the boys who hung around nearby. I climbed trees instead, huge firs from which freedom could be seen. I do admit though that, at around 14 years of age, I learned to smoke from 'friends' behind the gardener's shed.

The years between 1975 and 1976 were the run up to O levels. Having little experience of alternative opportunities, we worked and studied hard. Exam leave during the long, hot summer of 1976 was bliss. There were girls in bikinis clutching textbooks at the top of every fire escape in the boarding houses, taking care to stay hidden from view from the ground. It was a memorable summer holiday. I played (badly) for Somerset Ladies Wanderers cricket team who, without their own ground, were always treated to drinks in the pub following each game.

School rules were finally relaxed for those, like me, who stayed on to do A levels. We could have baths whenever we wanted and use the hot water urn in the kitchen. We could go out of the grounds at certain times in groups of three. We always assumed that was: one to be raped, one to help fight off the attacker and one to run for help. Not everyone stayed, a lucky few managed to swap to sixth form colleges nearer home but my parents forbade me to leave; the navy were supporting my expensive education.

In the holidays I either visited a French penfriend or hung around with several teenagers my own age who I'd known since Primary School, as naval families consistently bumped into each other and whom I regularly supplied with Gaulois. I became very disaffected with school, fluffing my A levels but just scraping the grades to go to Reading, my third-choice of university.

By then Mrs Thatcher had come to power but I remember little about politics; in the daily paper I followed only the cartoons and Ian Botham's exploits.

Carol   *1961 to 1979*

I was born in Mayday Hospital, Croydon. Apparently my dad wasn't happy because he wanted me to be born at home as he would have received a government benefit, so I caused trouble even before I was born! I was the third child. Dad was a coal merchant and mum stayed at home. I had a sister who was nine years older than me and a brother who was six years older. I was always the baby of the family, and in many ways, I still am.

My earliest memory is an incident when I was 4. At the house of a friend of my parents, I managed to fall in their fish pond. It was a Saturday evening and the gathered crowd were busy watching 'The Black and White Minstrel Show' on the TV, while I frolicked in the garden alone. I was probably playing one of my favourite games, imaginary showjumping. I was the rider on a lively horse, jumping over fences and other obstructions - obviously water jumps were not our forte! I got very wet and had to be stripped bare, wrapped in a towel - all of which was very embarrassing.

I went to Infants School when I was 5. I remember the navy blue cardigan my mum knitted for me and the piece of card that was pinned to it; it read 'Carol'. It was the only way people knew who you were, apparently. I loved school, and was soon reading books way above my age group. I had to go to the headmistress' office several times to prove to her my ability. Moving on to Primary School at 7, I enjoyed learning even more.

My only issue was the male teacher I had in my third year. Mr Saunders was ex-military and, consequently, a strict disciplinarian. In my mind's eye, he looked a bit like the actor Deryck Guyler, if you remember him. He insisted on teaching us to write in a specific way, and even I, a star pupil, got my knuckles rapped with his ruler, which he carried under his arm like a sergeant major's cane.

Fortunately my next teacher, in the fourth year, was a lovely young lady called Miss Heavens. Looking back, I think I may have had a small 'girl crush' on her - I wanted to be her. She always wore Scholl sandals and I remember desperately wanting a pair, not only because they looked nice, but I loved the flip-flop noise they made as she walked across the classroom. Unfortunately they were quite expensive and my mum's shoe budget never stretched that far. Most of the money went on sensible shoes and black plimsoles for games. New school shoes were always bought with 'a lot of growth in them'. A tightly packed wedge of cotton wool filled the space where the toes didn't reach. Normally, by the time they would have fitted me properly, they were close to disintegration!

As a small child I never really understood the idea of cooking, or should I say, food preparation. This was something that, with hindsight, must have taken up a lot of my mum's daily routine.

Shopping was done on a regular basis, at small local shops. At the bottom of our road we had a baker, a butcher and a fishmonger – all within easy walking distance, and as I got a little older, I was sent out on my bike for special errands. We didn't have a big fridge, so food was purchased when required as no money could be wasted on food that would go off before it was needed – no 'big shop' then.

I suppose the thing that stands out to me, is that nothing was 'quick and easy', in today's parlance. There were no instant meals, no microwaves and my mum's kitchen had none of the gadgets we can't live without now.

I suppose it was the anticipation of the preparation and cooking process that made mealtimes more special. Each time we sat down together as a family, we were, in some respects, taking part in a ceremony – appreciating the food that was placed in front of us, sure in the knowledge that every piece of food on our plates would need to be consumed before we could leave the table.

Everything had to be planned. Rice puddings couldn't be pulled out of nowhere – the rice was placed in milk to soak overnight, before being slowly heated in the oven the following afternoon. Chips were a real treat, as the potatoes had to be peeled, and cut into oblongs, before being placed in hot oil and fried – always a dangerous moment; it must have caused my mum a few nightmares. There were hours of steaming before we were presented with my dad's favourites, spotted dick or treacle pudding – oh, and the custard had to be prepared on the hob, carefully stirring the milk and custard powder. My dad would never accept lumpy custard, although he did like having the skin that formed on the top! Yes it was definitely a labour of love for my mum.

We weren't a well-off family, so money for food had to stretch quite a long way. It appears that there was a well-used system that my mum followed. It started on a Sunday, with a roast dinner. Monday would bring a cold version of that same meal – bubble 'n' squeak, obviously, mashed potatoes and pickles. Tuesday would sometimes be another small roast, based around anything that remained from Sunday, with some small additions. Wednesday would be a pie of some sort. Thursday would be a stew or casserole, and Saturday would be a fry up. Friday was always fish. I suppose that keeping the menus straightforward made it easier to buy for.

As my dad was a coal merchant, we always had an open fire burning in the grate, when the weather was cold enough. This was just in the back room where the majority of our living was done. The rest of the house wasn't heated – no central heating in those days.

The fire played several roles, including the times my dad came in from a cold, wet coal round, his jacket and trousers soaked by the rain. He would take them off and hang them over the backs of dining chairs and place them in front of the fire. I can still remember watching the steam rise off the garments and the air filling with the smells that that combination created.

The open fire was also the scene of another event that happened in our house in winter – toast! The skill of balancing a floppy piece of bread on the end of a ridiculously long fork and dangling it over the fire in the grate, will live long as a memory. Sometimes my efforts were not rewarded when I lost concentration and the bread fell into the flames. Jeopardy then entered the room, as one had to consider the pros and cons of trying to retrieve what was gradually turning into a pile of ashes. Would I be able to get another slice off the loaf that was sitting on the table without giving the game away? Only a wimp would consider using the grill that was available at the top of the cooker!

Outside of school I spent a lot of time playing with my brother who was 6 years older than me. We played football, cricket and tennis in the back garden and at the local park. I even had my own football boots! When left on my own, I also played 'schools', a game where I was the teacher and my pupils were all imagined. Janet Watscombe was my naughtiest student. That was my ambition at that time, to be a teacher.

My family were very involved in the local Conservative association, and the social club was the focus of our entertainment. There was a games room within the club, and that is where I learned to play table-tennis, bar billiards and darts, even at that early age! My Saturday nights in the 1960s harked back to an earlier age - bingo followed by a sing-song around the 'ol' joanna' – 'Roll Out the Barrel', 'My Old Man', 'It's A Long Way to Tipperary' and other classics were the highlights of the repertoire.

During my time at Junior School, being in a borough on the outskirts of London, we had several intakes of pupils from foreign countries, including the displaced children of Asian descent, created by Idi Amin. I never thought that this was strange or felt any ill towards them. I guess it was difficult for the teachers who saw their classes increase by up to 25 percent of pupils overnight. I don't think I ever saw the colour of these new children's skin, or if I did, it didn't change my opinion of them. These wonderful individuals with exotic names became some of my best friends, whose names and faces I can still fondly recall.

I remember sitting outside a pub with my family, on 20th July 1969, looking up at the moon, trying to see the astronauts that I knew were on it somewhere. I wasn't as enthralled with the event as my brother was; perhaps I was a little too young to truly understand the enormous nature of it, or wonder about the technology involved and the science it represented.

I took, and failed, the Eleven Plus exam, so entered the Comprehensive system. I believe I was in the first year that would follow this innovation fully. Just before I started High School in September 1972, my sister got married and for the only time in my life I performed the role of bridesmaid.

The first school I attended was the newly renamed South Norwood High School. My mum had been a pupil there in the 1930s and it had earned the nickname of the 'Portland Piggery' after the road it was near. It wasn't a very auspicious start, but any fears of it not being a good academic establishment were unfounded. I thrived in my academic studies, and the teachers, on the whole, were excellent.

I expect that in all schools there were teachers who relished the then accepted use of corporal punishment. Being the good, obedient girl I was, I never experienced this first hand or, indeed, bottom, if you see what I mean. These teachers were all men and they were very happy to dish out punishments, normally to boys, but a couple of rather obnoxious girls were often singled out too. Blackboard rubbers were thrown, rulers were used to inflict pain onto their bodies, extreme physical activity in the gym enforced - there were many ways to punish us. My third-year form tutor, who was also my English teacher, was infamous for his 'Mr Whippy', the instrument of torture that he proudly displayed on his desk, as a warning for any pupil who even thought about disrupting his classroom. I didn't let this concern me at the time, but looking back I assume that the experience of some of these children would have left permanent scars on their physical and mental wellbeing for years to come.

Life wasn't always easy for us. Things were quite bad during the 'winter of discontent' and the 'three-day week' period in early 1974. As the industrial action being taken included a miners' strike, my dad's main source of income was put in jeopardy. With coal supplies becoming limited, his ability to obtain and deliver 'the black stuff' diminished.

Looking back, I don't think that the worries that my parents were obviously suffering were allowed to impact on us kids, which is a testament to them. On a more personal level, I can remember sitting at the dining room table trying to do homework by the light of a candle while my mum juggled the family's requirements for food around the cutting off of the electricity and gas supply that became a part of our everyday life for that short time.

I learnt the guitar and joined the school folk group. I remember that we used to go out to local old people's clubs and perform for them, my first real experience of live music in front of an audience.

Music became an increasingly important thing in my life, and in 1976 my brother bought our first record-player and I can still remember the 5 LPs that were purchased to play on it! Before that acquisition, I had relied on an old reel-to-reel tape recorder. I would spend my Sunday late afternoons, listening to the charts on a radio, with a carefully placed microphone in front of it. I became an expert at recording my favourites each week, trying very hard to stop it before the annoying DJ started talking over them. The rest of the family had strict instructions not to disturb me during this crucial time, but I have memories of some tracks having added vocals from my mum, "Carol, do you want a cup of tea?", followed by me going "Ssshhhh"! Happy times.

I enjoyed sport and represented my school in netball, rounders, hockey and athletics. A friend of my dad, also a coal merchant, had a couple of horses in a small stables near my school, so I was lucky enough to spend time with them, grooming and mucking out. In return his daughter taught me to ride a little on a piece of waste ground nearby. It was a wonderful experience and one that was unusual to have in an urban environment.

Initially, based on my love of music, during 1973-4, I experienced my first example of fancying members of the opposite sex, although I didn't comprehend that feeling at the time. It was David Cassidy and Donny Osmond, at first, and then came the Bay City Rollers. That was the first time that my mum gave in to my pestering - she bought me a short sleeve tartan jumper with 'Rollers' emblazoned across the chest. I also wanted tartan trousers, but had to compromise - we got some old tartan from somewhere and cut it into strips and sewed it down the seams and on the turn-ups. With the addition of the rest of the material tied around the wrist, like a scarf, I would strut around thinking I was something special!

I was never allowed to go to a concert to see them live, I was too young, but for a while they had their own TV show called 'Shang-a-Lang', which was a must-see moment each week. I made sure I was home from school and in front of our small TV in plenty of time for this unrepeatable occasion - there were no video recorders in those days! My bedroom walls were covered with posters taken out of my Jackie magazines. Marc Bolan, Gary Glitter, David Essex, Alvin Stardust, Showaddywaddy, Mud - I loved them all!

At 14 I went up to the next High School, Selhurst, which was a girls' school that shared some facilities with the boys' school next door. This was the first time in my education that I had been in single-sex classes and, looking back, it was probably a good thing, as I may have had a tendency to get distracted by the boys.

There was a period of time, whilst at this school, that I experienced bullying. It was nothing serious, just name calling, but I often encountered a small group of fellow girl pupils who thought it was funny to taunt me as I walked to school every morning. Apparently I had 'bandy legs' and was ugly. I think I had the sense to realise that they were just jealous of how clever I was at my studies – their shouts of 'teacher's pet' were probably proved correct, as often one or two of my teachers would stop their car and offer me a lift to school as they were passing me on the street – it was ironic really!

Over Easter, 1976, I went on a school exchange trip to Bavaria and it was there that I had my first experience of being completely drunk. I was only 14, but there were older boys at a house party and we were all drinking beer. I don't remember much about it except one moment when I became aware of lying down with one of them. I don't think anything serious happened, but I wouldn't have realised it if it had. It wasn't until I was 16 that I fully understood the implications of sex - I was quite naive, but I think that was reasonably normal at that time. My group of friends knew boys were lovely but didn't fully grasp the 'mechanics'.

Back at school, my interest in boys flourished alongside my schooling. I achieved 9 O levels in 1977 but disappointed everyone when I only got 2 A levels in 1979. In the intervening 2 years, boys and disco dancing had become a real distraction. I frequented a club called Scamps, in Croydon, most Saturday nights, the six months before my A levels, underage of course, but it was such fun. We had all seen 'Saturday Night Fever', again underage, and thought we were 'it'. It relieved the drudgery of my Saturday job, working in Littlewoods, but I never had any money as I earned it during the day and spent it all the same night!

With hindsight, I am glad that I was part of a crowd that liked this strand of popular music, as perhaps other genres would have been more controversial and harmful to the relationship I had with my parents – here I am thinking specifically about punk. I can't imagine how the conversation would have gone if I had walked through the front door with a safety pin inserted somewhere on my body or a mohican haircut on my head!

During the first part of 1979, I was deeply in love with a boy called Marios, who won the heart of my mum too. I am sure she would have liked him to have become her son-in-law. He was a fantastic boy with lots of interesting pursuits, including amateur dramatics and disco dancing. His skill for the latter, led him to win prizes at dancing competitions which were very popular at the time and, I think, he even appeared on TV. We thought we would spend the rest of our lives together but I had to leave him behind, in the October, when I decided to take up my undergraduate studies.

Luckily, or unluckily, my 2 A levels were enough for me to be accepted by Southampton University to study history, and so I moved on to my next adventure. If fate had intervened, my life may have taken a completely different course, but I am glad that I pursued an academic path and independence, rather than becoming a young bride and the potential difficulties that would have presented.

Rosemarie (5) with her new dolls' house

Jo with Mum, Dad and baby sister

Maureen with her older sister

Jude aged around five years

Jocelyn (front, right) in primary school

Carol at 18 months

Rosemarie as a bridesmaid

Jo as a girl guide

Maureen (centre, cross-legged) age 12

Jude at Chi Hi aged 14

Jocelyn (12, with sisters) in her first 'flares'

Carol (16) with Butch

2 STEPPING OUT – EARLY ADULTHOOD

So I wonder whether these 'formative years' have left their mark. They are varied and have led along a variety of paths. Whether these paths have been influenced or not, who knows?

The next chapter we have called 'Stepping Out' as we progressed and left our family homes, some to university, some to workplace and/or get married and start our own lives.

We were all stepping out at various ages and at various levels of education and wordly experience. For some it was the early fifties, for others the seventies so the differences in world affairs was great. University was a dream for some and others almost just the next part of their education. The King dying in 1952 meant the start of the new Elizabethan age. 'Smog' was a new word in the English language, especially if one came from the London area. However, we all 'Stepped Out' into the unknown whether we were ready or not.

Joyce   *1947 to 1990*

1947-49

I was at Teacher Training College then went onto teaching at all types of school, starting with a Secondary Modern girls' school, then a Grammar school at Seven Kings.

1959

We were married. I stopped teaching for a while to have babies. After that came the Comprehensive Schools which were mostly quite large and also had both girls and boys. My own son was amongst the pupils.

Then I went to a Bilateral school, again mixed, although the boys and girls were seated on different sides of the class.

Time dulled my musical ambition but I did try to interest my two children instead. I had a boy and a girl. These were followed by one of each grandchildren. None of them turned out to be a Mozart. The piano was unused and was sold when we moved house.

1985

I then started to teach sailing. We instructed about six in each group, girls and boys. However eventually arthritis set in and I had to give it up.

The pressures of family and work meant that music became just the rare classical concert. When the family grew and left home I had more free time and joined a women's network through which I tried a number of workshops. 'Growing Old Disgracefully' was a group I then joined, written as g.o.d.

Now I have the privilege of preparing programmes from a large library of pieces collected in a music player. At last I have the pleasure of sharing 'my' music with friends.

Rosemarie   *1955 to 1958*

I went to an all-girls Training College when I was eighteen. I lived on campus sharing a room for the first year then upgrading to a modern building and my own room in the second. I have heard it said that teachers are now better trained because they do a minimum of three years. Right or not, the training at Bishop Otter was rigorous.

For the first two terms lectures were 9am to 6pm Monday to Friday and 9am to 1pm on Saturdays. There were assignments to do in addition to this. The same hours applied throughout the training but as assignments grew more demanding there were periods free from lectures. After the first term I came home very tired.

During the course there was block-learning of subjects such as maths and English and one had to pass an exam for each. There was some emphasis on anatomy and health and this was linked to child development, in my case learning about seven to eleven year old children as I was training to be a teacher of Juniors. Theory of Education continued for the two years with final exams for these. There was teaching practice of varying lengths in schools.

There was no student bar and we socialised by drinking tea in each others' rooms. Here I made a strong friendship group. We cycled to nearby seaside places. West Wittering was the favourite.

I became a bell-ringer at Chichester Cathedral and rang my first peel at Bosham. My interest in bell-ringing continued and after I left Chichester I went to practice nights in other places in areas I was visiting, including Truro Cathedral and Gloucester Cathedral. There was always a welcome. The bells in Farnham went to be recast and I went to Taylors in Loughborough to see the work in progress. There was a ring of twelve bells at Taylors, all light weight so the pace was very fast. I was pleased to have had that experience.

Back to the college years: a few things stand out. I passed my driving test when I was nineteen. An American battleship, the Iowa I think, docked at Portsmouth and as a year group we were taken to a reception on board. The tour of the ship was great but looking over the side was memorable, the deck being so far above the water.

There was the Suez crisis and I remember discussions on whether we would be conscripted if the troubles escalated.

The college had some treasures including a Henry Moore sculpture, a painting by Graham Sutherland and a Bernard Leach pot. These were on display and were passed daily. There is a Graham Sutherland painting in Chichester Cathedral. The college treasures were put in a secure place when the college became a university and in spite of requests through the college guild that these might be on view during reunion weekends it never happened.

Nearing the end of training I was offered a third year to specialise in maths but I wanted to get into the working world. I wanted to work in Bournemouth, just because I liked the place and wanted to live near the sea. This caused friction at home, my mother telling me it was up to me to put money into the family coffers as I had been reliant on my parents until I was twenty. My father kept out of the argument.

I applied to Surrey, Hampshire and London. The former two because there would be schools near home and the latter as a safeguard as there were, at that time, vacancies in London so I would not be unemployed. In those days one was initially employed by a local authority who then sent you to a school. I was accepted by all three and ended up at a village Primary School near Farnham working for Surrey Education Authority. I visited the school where I was to work to meet the Headmaster.

There was no pre-term staff meeting so on the first day of term I was shown to my classroom, given a register that listed the children who would be in my class and also a blank notebook in which I was to record my plans for the forthcoming week and each week thereafter. There was no National Curriculum. Primary school science was unheard of. There were no Teaching Assistants. The system worked.

I filled in my weekly plans but got no feedback. Children came to me from the Infant department as able as might be expected, with a range of abilities.

Occasionally an inspector from the local authority called in unannounced. The deputy Head taught the top class and quite a few were successful in the Eleven Plus. Class sizes were up to 42 and as I stood before my first large class there was only me and my personality to get me through. Again, I say the system worked and the children did learn. Most were polite and well-motivated. Every class had some who were a challenge and this never changed throughout my whole career. I was upset, and still am retrospectively, by the lack of help at that time for the very academically weak who would have benefited from attendance at a special school.

There were still Grammar Schools and I was now on the other end of the system, for on the days when pupils sat 'the Eleven Plus' teachers were sent to different schools to invigilate and then mark the papers. I found myself working beside teachers who had once taught me. Children who did not quite reach the pass grade could go through a process of interviews to fill the remaining Grammar School places. I was not involved but the Head where I worked was influenced by social background when asked about suitability of interview candidates!

Back home I was unsettled, for I disliked the restrictions, having known freedom! I loved the teaching and was confident I had chosen the right job. I went to evening classes once a week just for an interest, choosing pottery then tailoring.

I went back to ringing in Farnham. I met a man from the Aldershot tower. I stood him up on the first date for I had forgotten it was my mother's birthday and I was too scared of her to tell her I was going out on her birthday! (I could have put here that, out of great respect for my mother, I left the young man waiting!!). He did ask me again. We went on ringing outings together. He liked ancient history and one visit we made was to Stonehenge to see the sunrise on midsummer day. In those day you stood close to the stones. Druids handed round bread and salt.

On the day of my 21st birthday I arrived at work to find my classroom decorated and there were decorations all around the school. The staff provided goodies including cake to eat. There was a party at home for relatives then one for young friends.

Jo   *1955 to 1969*

1955

In Walthamstow there was a factory that made the new Ice Lollies, Shales it was called. When I worked in the laboratory I had to do hygiene tests on these. (I also did similar tests on sanitary towels, but that is another story).

Frank joined Solmedia. I would not say we were instantly attracted, but we were the only ones that were not Plymouth Brethren, therefore it was a bit 'them and us'. Frank did the deliveries and I always had a cuppa waiting for him when he got back. He had to deliver to various hospitals in and around London.

Also Nancy (Ann) Murphy joined us. She'd had polio as a child, and she still had one leg in irons. We became friends, we went out together. I felt she was quite sophisticated actually. We went to shows and parties. Mum and Dad did not like this - I stayed out later than they expected. There were no phones in those days, so on reflection they were quite worried, I think.

1956

One weekend Frank and I were invited to go to a Plymouth Brethren meeting. There would be tea afterwards at Miss Philips. She had taken over Nancy's job as the business's secretary and was also one of the Plymouth Brethren! She lived in a flat (half a house) in Upper Walthamstow, which was an expensive, posher part of Walthamstow. By this time I was interested in Frank so I got discreetly dressed up and he picked me up. Neither of us were converted to Plymouth Brethren, however that was our first date? I now wanted a proper relationship with Frank. He was nine years older than me but he was the one I wanted. So I left that job and – Frank followed!

I went to Lebus's, a furniture factory and offices. This was two buses away but also had a nice sports field where we could eat our sandwiches. They used to come round in the afternoon with a tea trolley with gorgeous cakes. They had big offices where I was employed to learn how to use the NCR machine. This was a National Cash Register; it was a large, extremely noisy accounting machine. There were about two dozen people employed there, even some men.

I was impatient. If I was going to learn anything I needed to get on with it. Others had started a couple of years earlier and were still not thought of as capable of using the machines regularly. It was slow going. The manager of the department had a little glass office in one corner, us workers had a big room, machines all down one side by the windows, the men at desks beyond the machines. One day I knocked on his door and gently complained that I was not getting enough training on the aforesaid machines. We had two supervisors. He told them to organise more sessions on machines for us three trainees. As a result, my name was mud in some circles, and hero in others!

When I felt fairly proficient I left and went to Brown Bros in Great Eastern Street. I now felt grown up, going by train, all the way up to Liverpool Street Station, I ended up as a checker going through the other girls' work finding errors. Frank and I were officially courting by then.

Can-can skirts with frilled underskirts were a rage in the 1950s - mine was black taffeta. Occasionally we younger ones wore TROUSERS. The women who had been in the forces during the war had found the usefulness of these garments and by the fifties we could wear them for casual wear, not smart wear.

I had two suits made for when I started work, a black barathea with gold taffeta lining, which I absolutely loved. The second was a sensible suit in a mustard-coloured plaid with brown lining. I was then set up for work.

1957
Grandma (Mum's mum) died on 20 January. I took Heather (aged 6) up to London for the day. Young children did not go to funerals then. It wasn't a good year. Grandad Peachey died 30 September.

Frank left Solmedia, they had hit hard times and because most of the others were Plymouth Brethren they looked after their own, so he had to go. He worked near me at Bethnal Green in a factory that made cords for curtains. He was in charge of the home-workers department. He was there for a couple of years.

When Frank and I first started courting we often used to go to his brother's place. They lived in a new flat in a tower block, well it was then, at six floors high. They were on the top floor. "Come and stand on the verandah" they would say. It seemed horrendous. But Iris, his wife, was a lovely lady and a good cook - spaghetti, which I had never had. I'd had it in a tin but not real like this. It soon became a favourite.

1958
During our courting days we had some regular haunts. The dog stadium was one. Walthamstow Stadium was renowned all over London. The one concession was that we went over to the posh side. I just enjoyed people-watching as much as race-watching.

We were saving up to buy a house. We found one we liked and that we could afford. It was expensive, £18.000, interest rate 7%. P.A which then over the next year or so went up to 15%. Never mind, Frank was earning the princely sum of £10 per week and my earnings were £5 10s. The house had been done up by a builder with a new bathroom downstairs and a loo!

We married on 26 July in the Registry Office, as we needed money to buy the house. Our honeymoon was to travel up to London, by bus, well two actually, to see Norman Wisdom in 'Charley's Aunt'. We went up and had a meal in Lyon's Corner House before the show. I remember Lemon Meringue Pie, which was new, the latest thing. Then we took the buses back to our new home, 22 York Road! We had to rent the house until my 21st birthday as I could not officially buy the house with Frank until I turned 21, which was the following November.

1959
Frank's Dad died in the January. His sister Pauline married in March; we had a little family gathering in our new house. Pauline and her new husband were renting a flat in Ilford, near Barkingside, where they both worked.

Then in August Joanna our first child was born. Of course in those days we could still work after we were married but had to leave work when expecting, I think it was eleven weeks before baby was due. I can remember suffering from morning sickness on the train going to work, and being sick out of the carriage window!

Frank and his brother Fred joined together and bought a car. It was an old banger. We had bits of car in our house while they repaired it. Then we shared it, Fred had it one week, we had it the next.

After I had my first baby I talked to my doctor about birth control. At this time the pill was in the news every day, but unfortunately she was a Catholic! She gave me advice about time of the month and withdrawal method but no mention of this new invention, the pill. I had to find the local birth control clinic myself. Eventually I was on and off the pill for the next thirty years. For me it was brilliant.

1960

Another death in the family. That's the trouble with larger families, people keep dying off. My Mum's sister's husband, Uncle Ralph, the one that lived at Barkingside, died on the 17th October.

1961

We decided to have another baby. A second child was born at home in those days unless there had been complications. So January, while I was giving birth, Frank was sitting in the dining room reading the paper and listening to Mrs. Dale's Diary! I never let him forget that, but that is how it was. He had taken Joanna to stay with Mum for a few days. Later that year we found out that Pauline, Frank's sister, who was my age, was also expecting. Unfortunately she and Liam were having problems. In the end she came and lived with us. She had a little boy in May. Both boys and Joanna were christened in October. I got a part-time job two evenings a week at the Stadium and Pauline got a Saturday job in the High Street.

1963

We decided to sell our house and buy a shop! This caused a bit of a stir. Our thinking was that Frank would still stay with his current employers, while Pauline and I would run the shop and look after the children. After a while we got buyers for the house, a very nice man and wife about our age. He was a bus driver and they had two young children. They seemed a very hard-working couple, we got on well with them. Then one morning our neighbour next door invited me in for coffee. She wanted to know why we were selling to 'them', it would 'ruin the whole neighbourhood'. "Prices will go down", she said. They did not want black people living next door to them!

Despite our neighbour's words we went ahead with the sale. I recently looked up prices in the area; houses were about £439,000 where we used to live.

Anyway we found a shop. It was in a built-up area, a corner shop with large old fashioned living quarters. It was ideal, no garden but a large yard that would be OK for the children. Pauline and I could run the shop and look after them while Frank would keep his job. It was quite exciting. Frank and his brother renovated the shop, making it ultra-smart. All we needed now was the customers.

On moving in and opening the shop, we immediately heard from local customers asking, "Are you going to still do deliveries?" Then we heard, "I've been taken to that new big store for most of my shopping." We didn't know about these new big stores called supermarkets in 1963-4. We'd been conned!

We could not understand why takings were not as good as the books showed. The customers were very nice on the whole, but we gradually learned why we had difficulties. The couple we had bought the shop from had a fair size delivery side to the business at some large flats nearby. The new supermarkets were just starting up in the area. Our trade was well down on that shown in the sellers' books. We hung on by the skin of our teeth.

Joanna started school in September. She did not like it at all. It was a big red brick establishment. Although she had two cousins there it still was not a success.

As we had planned Pauline and I worked in the shop and looked after the three children. Frank visited these new supermarkets to get us stock to sell (at a profit). Obviously we had proper wholesalers as well. Heather, my younger sister, was fourteen so she came and worked for us on Saturdays.

My Dad died 16th December. Mum and Heather came to stay for Christmas, which we had to celebrate for the children. They earned their keep that couple of weeks. Fred and Sheila had married that year.

1965

We sold the shop in June, just before we went bankrupt! Of course this meant we lost our accommodation as it was part of the shop. So we moved in with my sister Carole and Keith for about two months. Pauline moved into my Mum's with David, her son. We started exploring other possibilities. There was some talk of Carole and Keith going in with us and jointly buying a shop. We looked at a shop in Kidlington, just outside Oxford, a beautiful Georgian house and shop alongside. We went to see it, made an offer and then found out it was owned by Courage's Brewery. I don't know why the sellers did not know. They had been paying the Brewery rent for twenty-odd years but did not understand why. It was actually a tenancy which meant that the brewery still owned the land and building.

Anyway we had a joint interview with Courage's at their offices in Reading. As luck would have it, they had a shop available in Earley, a suburb of Reading, with three-bedroom accommodation. When could we start! We moved in on August 2nd and Frank joined to start as a manager at Arthur Cooper Wine Merchants on Monday 9th. We would live in a modern three-bedroom maisonette over the shop. We moved the day before Joanna's birthday and three days before Frank left Solmedia (he had returned to work for them a few years previously). So we postponed her birthday celebrations and cake until he came home to our new home.

We worked split hours, 10am to 2pm then 5pm to 9.30 until the start of December. Then for the Christmas period we worked 10am through to 9.30pm, without a break. We just had a drawer for the cash and it was coming up for Christmas, so bills were added up on the wrapping paper. Then for a few weeks it was all systems go. We were open all day, including Christmas morning 12 – 2pm. On Christmas Eve and Christmas morning the shop was full all the time; we hardly had any time off. Luckily Pauline was still with us so she was then official housekeeper and nanny. In an exhausting way we did sort of enjoy it. We worked for them for thirty years.

1966
Joanna joined the local school and I think enjoyed it. There was a progressive Head Teacher who was even getting the children to learn binary maths which confused me. We settled in well and got to know people. The boys went up the road in the mornings to a lady who had a big house and garden. She ran a playgroup in the mornings. They loved it. Then when Martin started school in January David stayed there until May when he started proper school himself.

1967
So we invested our money from the sale of the shop in another property, an older semi, just off the Basingstoke Road. We had felt a little unsettled at first because we heard through the grapevine that the company had no compunction about just 'locking you out' if there was any problem. I think we came pretty close at one point but managed to get through it. The couple (and their kids) who

had run the shop before us were now living in a flat in the same block, so we had heard about this directly from them. They seemed reasonably OK but were obviously struggling so we were glad we had invested in a house.

Colour television was coming in and we bought one.

1968
Miniskirts became the rage. Although I was married with a couple of children, I did shorten everything with glee! I had good legs I felt, so the shorter skirts went well with my beehive hairdo. Space was being explored!

The house we had purchased came in handy because Frank's brother, wife and young son decided to follow us from Walthamstow to Reading. They rented our house while they saved up for their own. They both worked in Reading and we looked after Colin, their young son. Fred became an insurance collector, while Sheila got a secretarial job.

1969
On the whole we enjoyed running the off licence, although the hours were long and we only had Wednesday afternoon off. We even worked Saturdays and Sundays (12-2pm and 7-9pm on Sunday). We had, at first, a fortnight off each year when a relief manager would come to the shop so we could have a holiday. Later on we had more time off with the shop closing all day on Wednesday.

Pauline worked at Cornhill Insurance Company which was just on the outskirts of Reading Cemetery Junction. Often I would phone her about eleven, then Concorde would come over me - we could not hear a thing. Then it travelled further and would go over her office. So we learnt to avoid that time for phone calls.

Maureen   *1958 to 1969*

1958-62

After a slight hiccup I began reading French at Liverpool University. All women students were accommodated in halls of residence, in shared rooms, with one bathroom to a corridor. There was no central heating. My room was known as 'The Fridge' because it was so cold. We had gas fires in each room, which were very good for making toast - a toasting fork was an essential piece of student equipment.

There were two or three payphones in a public place so long or intimate conversations were not possible. Communication with family was by letter, lucky people receiving one each week; mostly we lost touch with friends who went to other universities or stayed at home.

Rules were strict by modern standards : no men in rooms after six in the evening and a ten thirty curfew during the week which could be extended, by permission, to eleven at weekends.

By this time food was plentiful. The halls of residence served a cooked breakfast - if you were up in time, which I rarely was – and a hot dinner in the evening. On Sundays we were given 'supplies', which usually centred round a tin of baked beans or sardines, to give the cooks an evening off duty. There was a fair amount of choice in the canteen of the Student Union where we had our lunches. My lunches were an invariable cheese and tomato roll, an apple and a bottle of milk, the cheapest meal I could buy.

Because meals were provided (apart from lunch) the hall fees were high. I was lucky enough to get a full grant but even so there was very little money left for living expenses. Really needing the experience of going to

France, besides eating as cheaply as possible, I often walked home or got off the bus at the previous stage to save a penny on the fare. By the summer holiday I had saved enough to spend a month on holiday with my French pen-friend in the Pyrenees.

At University my clothes were still home-made, some by my mother, some by me. I began life there with a princess-line woollen dress with long sleeves, some tartan trews (all the rage), a pinafore dress in grey serge – and red gingham baby doll pyjamas! I began knitting my own sweaters. For Summer I had a dirndl skirt with big red flowers which I made at home, plus one in green & white that I had made at school and never worn. My shoes were flat heels for everyday, Louis heels for best wear at weekends. Hats were de rigueur in summer as well as winter.

The Salk vaccine against polio became available in England during my first year and students were the first cohort to be offered it. We were all very relieved because we had seen so many pictures of people living in 'iron lungs'.

In my second year I moved into a brand-new hall of residence where we had single rooms with a bathroom to every two rooms. It stood next to a church and was famously described as 'Cleanliness is next to godliness'. There was a kitchen on each corridor that was only used at the weekend as we still had evening meals provided on other days.

Every Sunday I joined a group of Methodist Society students for discussion, tea, and the evening service at our chaplain's church. Manse Squashes after the service were very popular as we were served lots of cake and often became very silly. There were occasional Socials too and it was at one of these that my future husband first took pity on a 'wallflower' then at the end of the evening asked me out on a date.

My final year was to be spent studying in France. During that time, we had to write a dissertation and end-of-year exams were designed to check that the work we submitted was our own. I went to Aix-en-Provence, a beautiful old town set in typical Mediterranean countryside. Studies were divided between the university and the school for foreign students which catered mainly for Americans and where the standard was way below what was demanded of us back home. Unfortunately I was not able to complete my time there because my mother died in the February and I came home.

1962-66
Unsettled by my mother's death I abandoned the Education course I was planning and went straight into teaching at a private school on the edge of the city with boarding and day pupils. I had a room at the school, very cheap and all meals provided, which was very useful as by this time I was saving up to get married.

Inexperienced and looking young enough to be a pushover, I found keeping discipline impossible. My head of department, coming from a career in educational broadcasting thought she knew everything there was to know about teaching, but did not think twice about dressing me down in front of the girls – one more time and I would have gone to the Union. I managed to last two years there, then left, got married and joined a Secondary-Modern-turned-Comprehensive school in an area that was rough but closer to my new home. After one horrendous term I resigned.

There were plenty of jobs going in computing and every applicant was on a par, that is, without relevant experience. Graduates, women as well as men, were particularly acceptable. I got a job as a programmer with IBM, which was much more fun and much less stressful than teaching.

I began work on the IBM 1440 series of computers, a data processing workhorse that had been around for a few years. The company arranged to fly me to Glasgow for a fortnight's training, allowing me to return home for the weekend. I went with another girl who had been taken on for a summer holiday job. Her parents were both academics and she was a gifted mathematician. I found the training interesting; the other girl found it a bit boring – it was too easy. She only made one mistake in the whole two weeks of the course! It was years before I realised that I was the normal one.

We had to learn the Assembler language which was only one step up from machine code. We laboriously wrote out the instructions on specially printed sheets; these were then handed to the punched card operators to type and produce the instruction cards. The next stage was for the instructions to be converted into machine code using a special program called a compiler.

In order to run a program, we had to make up a deck of machine code and data cards, feed these into the machine and hope that the program ran smoothly and gave us the right answers. If not, we had to alter the instructions by punching up new cards and going through the whole compilation process again.

When the Mersey Docks and Harbour Board took delivery of their brand-new System 360 computer (only the 3rd in the country) I went to work in their offices. They were housed in one of the 'Three Graces', the three imposing buildings that form the waterfront at the Pier Head. It had a huge marble entrance hall with a grand marble staircase leading to our first-floor office, a good test of fitness if you were late for work.

The programming team numbered about half a dozen, all men, half of whom were Liverpool supporters and half Everton fans. The day after a mid-week Derby was a nightmare of euphoria and gloom!

We had a training course laid on for us because the 360 had a different Assembler language from the 1400 series and worked in a very different way. For this we had to learn to count in binary (base of 2), octal (base of 8) and hexadecimal (base of 16).

In addition to punched card input and output, the System 360 had a wide printer, a typewriter that noisily produced messages from the depths of the system. It also had large, heavy removable hard disks that could be mounted on spindles in 2-foot square cabinets.

We were all working on the conversion of the existing programs so that they could be run on the new machine. These were not handling run-of -the-mill commercial data (orders, invoices etc) but things like pilotage fees for ships entering the docks. We programmed lots of reports, of course, but at least they had interesting subject matter.

1966-69

In preparation for the birth of my first baby I attended ante-natal classes with the National Childbirth Trust. My husband had found out about Natural Childbirth from a book that he had picked up to read on the train when travelling to London on business! Being across the city we had to drive to the classes and since I had scarcely driven after passing my test, he had to take me there. Luckily the teacher was happy to have husbands in attendance, which was extremely unusual at the time.

I was fit and well during pregnancy. At eight months I was still able to run for a bus or scrub the kitchen floor. Nevertheless, I had to leave work at six months. Employers' insurance did not cover accidents to a pregnant woman after that time.

I had hoped for a home birth but was strongly advised to have the baby in hospital in case of complications. When my husband arrived home from work, I told him that the contractions had started. He was due to attend an evening meeting. We discussed it and decided that it was safe for him to go as things were not progressing quickly. By the time he came home, the contractions were not much stronger but we did not want to get caught out in the middle of the night. He rang the hospital, who advised us to come in.

There seemed no hurry so we had our usual cup of cocoa before driving the seven miles into the city. When we reached the hospital, the doors were shut and locked. No one answered our knocking. We wandered around the streets, luckily deserted, looking for a phone box that had not been vandalised. The hospital told us they had kept the door open for us but had shut it when we did not appear. It could not be kept unlocked at night, they said, because otherwise the chairs were stolen.

Having delivered me safely, my husband was sent home to get a good night's sleep. He was with me from about eight next morning, only being sent out during examinations. The nursing staff were very interested in 'the lady who was doing the breathing'.

When they were satisfied that the delivery was imminent, they sent for the doctor, who gave the go-ahead. He refused to allow my husband back into the room saying, "He wouldn't want to be here". I insisted he did want to be here and lay there arguing. The doctor was adamant. Fortunately, when the doctor left and the midwife returned, she asked why he was not there and promptly went to fetch him.

After the birth he was so full of excitement that he called on several friends from church to tell them all about it. One lady said she had never before met a man who had had a baby!

I did not return to work but became a full-time mum. Being fifty or so miles distant from any family, and not having a phone in the house, I had no one to rely on for advice or help other than friends, who might have no more experience than I had. The 'Welfare' was a lifeline, a place to go each week to check on the baby's progress and to meet other mums from the area.

When my husband transferred his job to the firm's factory in Poole we bought a house on a new housing estate in Broadstone. Expecting my second baby I looked around for NCT classes but there were none. I had to prepare myself at home.

This time I was allowed a home birth. Two weeks overdue I underwent the indignity of castor oil and an enema to kickstart labour rather than go into hospital to be induced. I had a lovely midwife, though the baby was delivered by a trainee. When they arrived, they left the gas and air machine downstairs because they did not think it would be needed. It was not. My husband was once more present at the birth.

My mother-in-law had given up her two weeks' annual leave to come and look after our nearly two-year-old and the household generally. She brought coffee every day for the midwife who highly approved of 'this hotel'.

During the 1960s I wore shoes with stiletto heels and pointed toes, usually Clarkes. Nylons became seamless. Fashion became more varied through the decade, except for miniskirts. I made my own dresses as well as the children's clothes, gradually wearing shorter skirts until told my knickers could be seen when I bent down, an occupational hazard with small children. The fact that this was pointed out to me in church added to the embarrassment!

As a parent I cooked largely what I had been given as a child, using many of my mother's recipes. I had somehow by-passed all cookery lessons at school and having no particular interest in food I stuck with what I knew.

Jude   *1961 to 1976*

1961

My father took me to see the Youth Employment Officer in Bognor Regis who found me a job in London and some digs nearby.

On October 1st, I left home with one suitcase of clothes and some scant belongings. My father had met some strangers in the local pub at lunchtime who had been holidaying in Pagham (the next village) and who were returning to London that day. He had persuaded them to give me a lift. As I got in, my father thrust a £1 note into my hands.

It was a tiny car and I had to sit in the back between two others with the suitcase on my lap. The journey was silent until we got to London, when the husband asked for the address of the digs where I was expected. I handed him a scrap of paper. He drove around for at least two hours before they concluded that the address simply did not exist, so they took me home with them.

They lived in Ealing and were very kind, helping me to get to Crookes Laboratories in North Acton by a series of buses, feeding me and generally looking after me for about six weeks. Phone calls to my father for funds to pay them were unsuccessful. I was merely told I was on my own now and should pay them out of my wages.

Someone at Crookes managed to get me into the YWCA hostel in Acton. I wasted no time and upon discovering Brunel College of Advanced Technology (not then a university in its own right) was at the other end of Acton High Street, I wangled them to allow me to embark straight away on an external London University degree course in Biochemistry. I tried but failed to obtain a grant from London County Council who would only offer an 'estrangement from parents' grant after three years residency. I ended up doing a two-year sandwich non-honours external degree course, alternating between pharmacological research at Crookes and attending college.

In late 1961 I also started studying piano with Fiona Cameron, daughter of Basil Cameron a well-known conductor, and wife of Derek Simpson an equally well-known cellist with the Aeolian String Quartet. It was at her house that I was introduced to Yehudi Menuhin who gave me a lesson on how to play a Bartok sonata for about 40 minutes. My grandmother wanted me to become a concert pianist. My father told her she was wasting her money.

There were 5 grand pianos at the hostel dotted around and I used to get up at five a.m. to practise for three hours before getting a bus to North Acton to get to Crookes or to walk up the High Street to college. By cooking Sunday lunch for everyone around at the hostel (a lot of girls went home for weekends) I could get 12s .6d off my rent. I played the little organ in the chapel for the hymns at the Sunday morning service for another 2s.6d and then after lunch would catch a trolley bus to Shepherds Bush and a tube to Bond Street to attend the Sunday afternoon matinee concerts at the Wigmore Hall, courtesy of free tickets delivered to the hostel each week and in which no-one else was interested. I well remember attending the debut recital of John Ogdon who has recently died. He was brilliant.

There was a good badminton court at the hostel and I became fairly proficient at the game. There was a Badminton Club to which men could come in and play on Saturday afternoons (men otherwise absolutely forbidden to enter the hostel at all) and which I joined. I enjoyed that immensely.

1962

I did get a scholarship to the Royal Academy of Music but provisional upon my passing at good grade, music at A level - a subject of course I had not taken.

I joined the CND and went on the Aldermaston March with Bertrand Russell, ending up in Trafalgar Square where I climbed a lion and dipped into the fountains before being arrested. I was taken to Bow Street police station in a paddy wagon and spent the night there before being released without charge.

I went home for a weekend this year. My stepmother was always pleased to see me. There was a Formula I motor race on at Goodwood Motor Racing Circuit at which my father was a steward. He had said I could join him in the pits, which was uncharacteristically nice of him. I cycled over there but arrived too late to be allowed under the track to get into the pits, so I watched the race from the other side along with all the other punters.

I was right bang at the fence just beyond the chicane. I saw Stirling Moss crash. It was spectacular and horrifying. I saw the ambulances arriving and him being carried off. I saw them clearing away the debris of his racing car. Although the race had been cancelled, strangely none of us at the course that day knew how serious this crash was until we got home and heard about it on the six o'clock news. It finished his career.

That year I recall was the year of the Cuban Missile Crisis. I remember working on some drug experiment at Crookes and Dr. Ashford, head of Pharmacology, planning what we would do if we all had to leave London in the event of WW3 and where we could set up a temporary laboratory.

1963

Crookes was taken over by Phillips, a Dutch firm who decided to relocate it to Basingstoke. There was only room for one research laboratory assistant there and as I had no particular wish to go to Basingstoke, I gave up my place to a chap called David who was keen to make his career in drug research.

I started to look for another job and answered advertisements in the London Evening News and Standard. I thought vaguely of journalism. I applied to the BBC but received no reply. Then I was called for interview by two places at the same time on the same day. One of the interviews was for some kind of trade magazine and the other from some other place to which I had no recollection of applying. I phoned up the latter to change the time of the interview and politely asked what the job was for. I was frostily told that as I had applied for it I ought to know.

The interview with the trade magazine was uninspiring and dull so I hopped on a bus from the City to Oxford Street to get to Stratford Place for the next interview. I still had no idea what this job was about but, intrigued, I went anyway. Stratford Place is opposite Bond Street tube station and I was due at No. 5 at 3.00pm. As I rang the bell, I noticed a brass plate on the door which said 'Mortimer Silverman Solicitors'. I had no idea what a solicitor was, other than someone to whom my grandmother went to make or change her Will.

I was ushered into a large room dominated by a huge mahogany desk and was seated on a chair some yards away opposite my interviewer - a small bald man with wire rimmed glasses and whose head only just came over the top of the desk. That morning, the button on my skirt had come off and my skirt was now held up by a huge nappy pin. As I sat down, the safety pin came undone and the pin end started working its painful way into my side. I wriggled about to get it out to no avail and sat there trying not to writhe in absolute agony. The more I wriggled, the deeper the pin penetrated.

I was also fascinated by the appearance of the man opposite me whose head was darting about just visible over the top of the desk and who was droning on incomprehensibly. "I don't mind training you" he said. "I will correct your first mistakes and even some second ones but if you make the same mistake three times you will be asked to leave. Is that clear?". I nodded. "Good" he said. "You can start on Monday at 9.0'clock".

I left the interview with absolutely no idea what the job was for, but I turned up the following Monday and was introduced to my secretary. What? A secretary? For me? I was shown my room or my office and noticed it had my name on the door. Crumbs!

My secretary said, "Your post is on your desk".

Post? "What sort of post?" I asked trying to imagine a clothes post or a gatepost on top of a desk.

"Your MAIL" the secretary barked, rolling her eyes.

"You mean LETTERS?" I asked. "You mean someone has written to me already? How did they know I would be here? What have they written to me about?".

All the secretary could say was that I would soon find out and God Help Us.

It turned out I was a debt collection clerk, suing defaulting customers in County Courts all over the country who had fallen into arrears with their hire purchase or credit sale agreements, getting judgment against them, repossessing the goods and sometimes making them bankrupt. I was taken in hand by the Managing Clerk who taught me a lot. I became hooked on the law and never looked back.

I wanted to qualify. To embark on a law degree course meant I needed Latin A level so that was out. In those days, obtaining articles for a five-year apprenticeship was coupled with passing the Law Society Qualifying exams Parts 1 and II, which was not very easy. Even if one could find a solicitor willing to take on an articled clerk, the practice of paying a premium for the privilege of being articled was still prevalent and the period of articles was usually unpaid or paid so poorly one needed a good private income.

There had very recently been founded the Institute of Legal Executives offering part time law courses with examinations leading to an Associateship after three years in qualifying employment and a Fellowship after eight years. With no alternative, I signed up, went to night school three evenings a week, undertook demanding correspondence courses and studied law in all my spare time.

I left the YWCA this year and also got a part time job serving drinks in the Starlite Club in the basement of Number 5 Stratford Place, let out by Morty Silverman to a chap called Maurice, whom I had met taking down the rent demands. I would go there after night school, 9.30 to midnight. I was constantly tired but I needed the extra income in order to pay my share of the rent on a flat in

Barons Court I was now sharing with two girls I had met at the hostel – Anna and Rosemary.

One evening at the club I was serving drinks to two men sitting at the bar who were discussing what I assumed was a film script. It was very exciting and so much so that I broke into their conversation to say sorry but I could not help overhearing what they were talking about and asked them what the end was? Startled, they moved away at once glaring at me menacingly, which I considered rather rude of them.

A day or so later, as I was catching a 73 bus in Oxford Street to Hyde Park Corner (tube from there to Barons Court), I was hauled backwards by two men from the tailboard and shoved into a car behind, driven by someone I had often seen in the club and who I was later to identify as a leading East End gangster- not one of the Kray twins but an infamous rival.

He drove me to a mansion block in Mayfair and ushered me into an enormous penthouse apartment expensively furnished but empty. I was told to sit down on one of the sofas. He sat opposite, pulled out a gun and shot it into a cushion on another chair. The cushion exploded sending feathers all over the room and there was a very pungent scorching smell. He said that that was what would happen to me unless I kept quiet. I sat still as a mouse hardly daring to breathe.

He asked me how much I knew. Puzzled I asked, "Know about what?".

"The raid tonight" he replied.

"What raid?"

He eventually started laughing when it became clear to him I had no idea what he was talking about. He pushed me into a bedroom and said, "This is where you are staying tonight, my girl. We can't take any chances". He locked the door behind him.

I must have fallen into a deep sleep because the next thing I knew daylight was coming through the curtains. The flat was empty. There was no sign of my captor. The door had been unlocked and there was a £10 note on the coffee table in the room, which was covered with feathers and which still smelled of burning. I escaped into the street and hailed a taxi to take me to Barons Court.

The newspapers that morning were full of articles and pictures of a well-known jewellers' in Old Bond Street where a daring heist had taken place the previous night. Diamonds, gold and other valuables had been stolen. Whilst reading how the raid had taken place, I realised that it followed exactly the film script I had overheard. I decided to hand in my notice to Maurice, but the night I did so was also the day I heard the news of JFK's assassination.

Next to Barons Court tube station there was a small newsagents', tobacconist and general store and I would often call in there on the way home to get something for supper. On several occasions I was in the shop when Rudi Nureyev came in – sometimes still in his leotard. Just round the corner in Talgarth Road was Margot Fonteyn's studio house - one of a series of houses with amazing floor length windows and which are still there today.

At Barons Court we had an excellent view of the tennis courts at Queen's Tennis Club. Our flat had a balcony which overlooked them.

As I was now living in a flat I decided to go home and pick up my belongings from my parents' house. A former member of our extensive gang was also living in London working as an estate agent in St John's Wood and had a car. He was willing to give me a lift back to London with all my stuff. I phoned my stepmother who was more than willing for me to stay for the weekend even if my father was not so keen. She and I had always got on very well. I particularly wanted to retrieve the beautiful small blue wicker chair my mother had given me for Christmas the year she had died and of course all my books and other belongings I had been obliged to leave behind two years previously.

I caught a train down because Jeremy worked on Saturdays. As I got off the bus - the bus stop was very conveniently at the end of our drive - I noticed a thick plume of black smoke swirling its way upwards and skywards and which seemed to be coming from the back of the house. I walked up the drive and there on the back lawns was a big bonfire. On the bonfire were all the belongings I had come down to collect, including the little blue wicker chair, all my books and other 'treasures'.

I was aghast. My father merely said, "Lay not up for yourself treasures in this world".

I caught a train back to London and did not stay for the weekend as planned.

I was now nineteen and had reached the end of my teenage years.

1964

I had left Mortimer Silverman and was now at Cripps Harries Willis & Willis at No.1 New Square, Lincoln's Inn. Anna, one of my flatmates at Baron's Court was engaged to Malcolm, who was in the Household Cavalry. The three of us used to go and see him when he was sitting on a horse in a sentry box outside St James's Palace and feed the horse apples and chewing gum to try and make Malcolm break his expressionless face. He was, however, too well trained to succumb to such taunts and remained motionless and utterly still during these assaults.

Whilst at Cripps Harries, I had discovered some ancient title deeds for No. 1 New Square which gave the occupier the right to tether one's horse to the iron railings in the square. Malcom used to exercise Hannibal, the drum horse early in the mornings and frequently rode him through Lincoln's Inn Fields. I persuaded him to ride Hannibal one morning to the main entrance of Lincoln's Inn and allow me to ride the horse the very short distance into New Square, (he was a huge horse and Malcolm, trembling with nerves, had to give me several leg ups before I could get into the saddle) and to let me tie Hannibal up at the particular iron railings where the senior partner used to park his car.

I had timed this to perfection, for only a minute after I had tied the horse up, Storry Deans, the senior partner, arrived and had an apoplectic fit when he saw the horse. He got out of his car and fumed and raged, "What is this bloody horse doing here?".

I told him that we had the right to do this and I was merely exercising the right. Malcom, hovering nearby, untied Hannibal, sedately walked him out of the Inn and rode him back to Wellington Barracks before he could be caught and court martialled. A childish exploit but great fun as no-one liked Storry Deans, who once told me to stop wearing perfume as it was too distracting for the men in the office. In retrospect I may have been bit heavy with Estee Lauder's Youth Dew or Worth's Je Reviens.

1965
I was 21 and had a party at Baron's Court.

1966
I was bridesmaid at Jackie's wedding in Devon and having passed all the exams had gained my Associateship of the Institute of Legal Executives.

1968
After a stint at Gaster & Turner at 81 Chancery Lane as a High Court litigation clerk specialising in Trade Union law, I finally ended up at Gilmore Tylee & Naylor at No.14 Essex Street, where I was not only offered free articles but also paid whilst on study leave. The senior partner there wanted me to qualify so that I could become a partner. It was my lucky break.

This year saw my second 'being held up at gun point.' I was interviewing someone who I thought was a client when he pulled out a gun on me after having demanded title deeds which were not his. Fortunately I was rescued by my principal and another man who floored him, resulting in the gun going off and the bullet ricocheting round my office and lodging in the ceiling, bringing down a shower of ancient plaster.

It was also the year my stepmother telephoned me to say she was leaving my father and taking my two half-sisters with her. He had become impossible to live with, hurling dinner plates at the walls and ranting and raving like the lunatic he had perhaps always been.

My Deed of Articles had been signed up with Paul Gilmore and registered at the Law Society in Chancery Lane. The contract was generous for the five-year period of apprenticeship and even catered for annual salary increases. The next few months were spent developing skills in copyright and contract law in the music industry. Amongst our clients were Hot Chocolate, The Strawbs and other musical impresarios such as Norrie Paramour and burgeoning pop groups of the day.

I was now living in Caterham, Surrey, having decided to get onto the property ladder. Janie, one of my '5 J' friends had lent me the money for the deposit on a two-bedroom flat just up an extremely steep hill from the station. I became incredibly fit!

1969

I watched Neil Armstrong land on the moon on 21st July this year on a black and white television I had bought for my flat in Caterham.

1970

I applied to go on the course for Part 1 of the Law Society Qualifying Examinations in August, with the exams in February 1971. In August, I started at Law school, which was at Lancaster Gate. At 26 I was older than my classmates, all men. The course was for six months (actually only. 96 working days) and we studied all core law subjects which law degree undergraduates took 3 years to get through (Graduates in law from approved universities were exempt from taking Part 1).

It was an extremely intensive course and there were a number of dropouts. From starting off with a class of 25 we were down to 18 or 19 by the end of the course. One was obliged to pass all seven heads at one sitting. Only rarely was anyone allowed a re-sit and if they were, it had to be in only one head and one had to prove extenuating circumstances to explain the failure. One could always of course take the whole lot again provided one's principal allowed it. Fortunately I passed all heads at the one sitting, even gaining a couple of distinctions, due no doubt to having previously studied the subjects.

Earlier this year I had gained my Fellowship of the Institute of Legal Executives, having come top of the country for Equity & Trusts, and for the exams which I had taken anyway 'just in case'. Having secured articles, it was no longer necessary to take these exams or even to gain the qualification but I thought I may as well.

1971

Just before exam time in February I was told that the practice of Gilmore Tylee & Naylor had been sold and was now merged with a firm of solicitors in Upper Regent Street, but a specific term of the sale contract was that the purchaser should honour the terms of my contract and deed of articles. Exams over I duly turned up to meet the partners of my new firm. Only Mr Naylor (one of Paul Gilmore's two partners) and myself had joined it.

I had inherited (from the other former partner who had gone off to head up a prestigious property company) all of the music industry clients and was the only person specialising in management and recording contracts etc. My little 'practice within a practice' flourished very well. I was well acquainted with some of the big names in the industry and had great fun attending concerts and recording sessions with them.

My father's mother died. She had phoned me a few days beforehand saying she hadn't been feeling too well. "But I don't want you rushing down here". She had apparently told her next-door neighbour "My time is up. Please take all the Victoria plums and anything else in the garden when I'm gone. I don't want it going to waste", went to bed and promptly died.

1972

Going into work in July one morning, I came across Mr Naylor incongruously sitting on a sofa on the pavement in Upper Regent Street surrounded by all his office paraphernalia. Ashen-faced, he told me he was waiting for a removal van to take him home with his belongings. He was clearly in a state of shock and could hardly speak. He just shrugged and waved me inside the office.

I went to see the senior partner and asked him what on earth was going on. 'The merger contract has been rescinded by Paul Gilmore" he said. "Why?" I asked. "Misrepresentation" he replied.

I shall not, here, go into this - it is a story for another time - but this was indeed very serious news. I was a term of a contract that was no longer in existence, the full implications of which hit home and hard. "Oh, by the way" the senior partner added "Paul Gilmore has resigned and is no longer practising. He has gone to live in Switzerland."

I was now articled to no-one. I had no principal. This was so grave and so potentially life-changing that without being asked I sat down. We both sat in silence and then he said, "I was thinking of getting a new articled clerk. I'll take you on if you like but you'd better get yourself off to Law School pretty damn quick before I change my mind or my partners change it for me - I mean like right now. I'll see you through your finals but that will be the end of it, OK?".

I rushed up to my office and made several telephone calls. I just managed to enrol for the August intake at Law School for the six-month Law Society Part II Qualifying Examinations in February 1973, only discovering much later that I was six months too early. In those days one had to leave two complete years between the taking of Part 1 exams and starting a Part ll qualifying course. This meant that I had to repeat the whole two years all over again but I did not realise this until the exams were over.

I remember the miners' strike this year.

1973

In February it was exam time again. The Law Society exams in those days were held in Alexandra Palace - a vast area with a glass roof and pigeons flying inside. Two exams a day, three hours in the morning and three hours in the afternoon, Tuesday to Thursday. There were only six heads to pass this time but the same applied - all heads to be passed at one sitting. Having sat the exams, I went back to the office and was told I could use it as a base while I hunted for a new position elsewhere but only for six weeks. I attended several interviews and eventually took the position offered by Kingsley Napley & Co.

Just after Christmas the three-day week came into operation - a national electricity-saving enterprise. I remember going to bed at 9.00pm with only candles for light and hot water bottles for warmth.

1975

My father died aged 60 in St. Richard's Hospital in Chichester. He had previously been taken to Graylingwell, the local 'looney bin' for about six weeks before they decided he was clinically, not mentally, ill and transferred him. St Richard's were unable to diagnose his condition and after he died there had to be a post mortem. The cause of death was TB. No doctor in 1975 had ever seen a case of TB. On my last visit to him in hospital sometime in early October he told me "I'm sorry I was such a rotten father".

Having repeated my two years I was now formally admitted to the Roll. Better late than never

This year too, I was made a partner of Kingsley Napley - their first, and only the second woman partner in a London or even a national firm of note - which made all the press. (Blanche Lucas had been a partner of Theodore Goddard for ten years and held the first position but no other woman had been appointed since then to any firm of solicitors).

Jocelyn   *1978 to 1990*

I chose to read Cybernetics and Psychology at Reading University because the combination sounded thought-provoking and was somewhat surprised to discover, on arrival in 1978, that Cybernetics was solely electronics, maths and control engineering. The advertised links to human mental processing were not being implemented that year as the instigating tutor had left. However, both departments were in the same building and I saw no reason to choose one subject over the other. They were both interesting in their own way, though Cybernetics, where I was one of three girls amongst forty boys, was much harder work.

The academic programme quickly took second place to a full social life which progressed from being shocked rigid in the first term by the sight, one morning in hall, of a boy from downstairs in his dressing gown to sharing my room, on occasion, with other similarly inexperienced young men.

There was a rich variety of sports. I joined the rowing club and played cricket. Also the ENTS team at the Students' Union kept everyone well entertained with bands, discos and comedians and I graduated from a schoolgirl passion for glam rock to reggae.

At university the food was better and, once I had moved out of hall and started to cook for myself, served in healthier quantities. Even though I shared a house we only rarely shared meals, everyone's daily routine was different. However, it wasn't a surprise to see everyone after a Saturday night gig at the Students' Union in the queue for the kebab van. As for parties, we had many with different themes but a pot of chili con carne with French bread or rice was a staple whenever any large gathering was planned.

Punk was big at the time but, except for dressing in torn denim, somehow it passed me by. I couldn't be doing with all that spitting.

Over time, I acquired a series of brightly coloured outfits in red, gold and green for going out to gigs in and, in addition, a pair of silver stretch (thanks to the introduction of Lycra) trousers. All were accessorised with, of course, extensive supplies of kohl and black eyeliner. However, kept at the back of the cupboard was a completely different outfit for visiting Henley Regatta each year with my father – a shirtwaister cotton dress, a straw boater and sandals with heels.

I finally passed my driving test in 1980 at the age of 20 but, without funds for a car, chose to ride cheap, underpowered motorcycles. I even joined the university motorbike club where I learned to drink pints of beer. Everyone paid for their round and, as I had to pay 30p a pint for each of the lads, there was no way I was going to let them get away with buying me half measures.

Despite Margaret Thatcher's election and reports of IRA bombs in the big cities our everyday conversation was dominated by the latest episodes of the Hitch Hiker's Guide to the Galaxy radio show. There was some political awakening though. I was very interested in alternative technologies and started going to demonstrations in support of CND and Greenpeace. In my final year I also visited the Greenham Common women's peace camp with a lad only to find that, as a male he wasn't welcome.

I remember more about the festivals I attended, - listening to Hawkwind play Silver Machine for hours on end before the sun rose at Stonehenge was a highlight – than the final university exams. The academic year finished with me going to Glastonbury Festival for the first time. I came back to discover I had just missed the boundary for a 2:1 degree. Not surprising really.

Getting a second-class degree meant settling, in 1981, for my insurance offer from the university's jobs milk-round, working with a government systems contractor as a technical author. At the office there was a clear division between genders, the men wrote the computer programs, the women documented them and wrote the user manuals. To this day I have never understood why the programmers weren't expected to document their own work, doing it for them was unbelievably tedious.

I preferred to wear bright colours and slacks or even patchwork cotton trousers (purchased at the summer music festivals I regularly attended) to work, and I fought, often unsuccessfully, against the unwritten company dress code. My stock response that, as a junior back-office staff member who was never in sight of the customers or the management, dressing smartly was unnecessary fell on deaf ears. This was an infuriating, double standard as, so long as it was not dirty jeans, the male programmers who worked along the corridor could wear what they liked!

I stayed in touch with several friends from university and, like many other young people at the time, regularly hitch-hiked to meet them for pop concerts, camping trips and festivals. After some months at work I was able to give up hitch-hiking as I could now afford petrol and my grandmother passed on her car, an early Mini, to me.

One Sunday I even went back to Greenham Common in support of the women (it was a big decision given the sensitive nature of my job linked to the hardware that operated RAF fighters) only to have to cry off work the next day to recover from the extremely impressive effects of unknowingly being given hash cake by another visitor.

During this short 18 month period of my life I shared a house with other young people in Farnborough, some in the same line of work and some employed by the local hospital. At one housemate's birthday party I met a young nurse trainee who, though I didn't realise it at the time, I would eventually marry. We took to spending time together, possibly through force of circumstance as the Mini had failed its MoT and I was now driving an elderly Morris Minor convertible that often broke down. However, as things grew more serious he offered to take me out to dinner in the early eighties. There was an exciting new restaurant in Aldershot that we wanted to try out, one of the first McDonalds outside London!

Late in 1982 I escaped from the boring job with the offer of a research post in the Psychology Department at Surrey University, working on creating software to simulate human behaviour in disasters so as to create better evacuation plans. This research project had been triggered by the King's Cross fire amongst other recent sad events.

The first personal computers became available and I was lucky enough to have my own hard disk drive. It was the size of a large suitcase and I kept it under the desk where I could rest my feet on it. I enjoyed both the work and the social opportunities linked to a job at a university so much that I signed up to do a PhD studying what was it about computer software, especially computer games, that made them so addictive.

I lived all this time in a series of shared houses which made for more than a few excellent parties and eventually ended up living as a couple with Rod, the aforementioned nurse, who had now qualified and was working at the nearby Guildford Hospital. One of the houses we shared was with members of the university motorcycle club. I graduated to a larger motorbike, a Honda CBX550 on which I took Rod to that year's Glastonbury festival and, months later, eventually agreed to marry him.

In 1985 Rod and I moved to a small flat in Slough which we purchased with a large mortgage and contributions from both sets of parents and continued to live cheaply. We were careful about sharing equally and always took the household chores of cooking, shopping and cleaning etc in turn.

When it was my turn to cook, we benefited from the wider range of ingredients becoming increasingly available in the supermarkets and I mostly cooked spicier versions of my mother's weekday recipes such as bolognaise, chili con carne, curry or kedgeree. Though we bought the mince rather than mincing the leftovers from the Sunday joint as Mum would have done in the 1960s.

When it was Rod's turn he preferred to cook from frozen and, as he will only do exactly what it says on the packet, it took years of suffering cold pizza and chicken kiev with the centres still icy to get him to understand that, when the packet says 25 minutes at 200 degrees, the oven must be heated to temperature first.

That summer, in July, we hitch-hiked to the South of France for a holiday. The journey was memorable for the fact that throughout the day, in different vehicles, we all listened to Bob Geldof's sixteen-hour Live Aid Concert. Nearly a year later, in May 1986, Rod and I were married from a church near my parents' house in Bath. One of the highlights of living in Bath is the number of buskers and we were delighted that a group of folk musicians I spotted in town agreed to play at our reception the next day.

Rod worked as a nurse in Accident & Emergency at the hospital in Slough and I continued to commute to Surrey University, where I was enjoying collecting data in local Primary Schools for my PhD, travelling widely on the motorbike. Unsurprisingly I soon became pregnant, and we took up the opportunity of a promotion for Rod and a move to a small house in Southampton. It became clear that I would not complete my doctorate before the baby arrived and, indeed, I spent some hours of early labour printing out lengthy drafts on fanfold paper.

Computers had become small enough to get into the home but printing and storage was erratic. I once lost an entire chapter when a box of floppy disks fell off my bike and were run over.

In September 1987 our first daughter arrived weighing roughly the same as the required three copies of the PhD thesis. Rod was present at her birth as fathers were now welcomed on the labour ward. Now with a baby, expecting to have more and at a loose end, I decided on a career change and, having enjoyed myself conducting research in Primary Schools, applied to train as a Primary School teacher only to be rejected. Apparently I was thought overqualified. The next year I was finally awarded my doctorate and applied again for teacher training but at the Secondary level, choosing physics as my specialist subject for computing courses were few and far between.

1989 was a hectic year. In the summer our son arrived and I juggled teacher training and child care. We had acquired an elderly VW camper in which all four of us stayed as we toured England, Scotland and later, one memorable year when Rod was between jobs, managed a long summer break around Europe. But travelling in the van with its tendency to break down whenever you least expected it was always highly unpredictable. Yet it was with sad hearts that we decided to sell it when the garage finally ruled that it required a new engine.

After qualifying I was appointed to a teaching post in a local Sixth Form College which had the added bonus of running a nursery nursing course, and we were fortunate in securing newly qualified nannies without it costing us a fortune.

I had to spend more on clothes though, 'smart casual' was the required dress code and your clothes got so dirty when teaching in the rooms that still had blackboards. Fortunately, this was before schools started insisting on business suits for both staff and sixth form. As a science and technology teacher, I have never understood the purpose of this – even these days anything you wear to school is instantly wrecked by the need to crawl around, whether getting kit out of ancient cupboards, setting up complex experiments or trying to persuade a recalcitrant computer or whiteboard to work.

Over the next few years I also became more aware of both local and national politics. My mother was a Tory town councillor and Rod's father was a Labour one. We were delighted to hear in 1989 of the fall of the Berlin Wall and, whilst being unprepared to tolerate violence, were supportive of the protestors at the 1990 Poll Tax riots. At the time though, I was dismayed by the vicious Tory and Labour attacks on what, until then, had been progressively more successful Green Party policies and lost faith in politics and politicians.

Carol   *1979 to 1991*

Packing up, getting ready to move down to Southampton in early October 1979, was a moment of mixed emotions. There was great excitement at what the future held, but this was tinged with the sadness of having to leave behind lots of very good friends, and in particular, my boyfriend. I was looking forward to my studies which would lead to a history degree.

I didn't appreciate how lucky I was to be able to go to university, not because of my academic abilities, but because of the financial commitment. Coming from a working-class family who never had much money, I was fortunate to get a full grant from the government, that covered the university fees and my accommodation. I still had to find the money to pay for my food, books and other incidentals. My parents were a great source of support and it must have been difficult for them to find the extra funds I required. It was an early lesson in how to live on a restricted budget, which was a good one to have.

I had secured a room within a hall of residence which was a modern building, which had certain comfort benefits, like central heating. Each accommodation block was split into sections that housed seven students, each person having their own room and access to shared bathroom facilities and a kitchen. I was happy with my own little room which had space for everything I needed. I quickly made friends with the six other young ladies I shared facilities with and one of them was also a history student, so she became my best buddy. It was strange not having my parents to look after me, and even weirder that mum wasn't there presenting me with my meals. The university had a student canteen that became my favourite eatery, not very healthy living, but substantial and reasonably priced.

After the initial excitement of Fresher's Week, which had culminated in a concert by Slade, which was excellent but very loud, it was straight into the business of lectures, tutorials and long hours of research in the library. There was also some time for boys, although I suppose, by now, they were men. There was a group of third year male students in the apartment below ours, and they soon started 'calling' on us. There was an invitation from two of them, to myself and my friend Liz, to join them for a pub crawl - we accepted, and I suffered the biggest hangover I had ever had! I gravitated towards one of these 'men' and we 'became an item'. His name was Gary and he was in the final year of his Electronics degree. We were to stay together, on and off, for about four years. He was a complex character and our relationship, at times, was challenging.

At the end of the first term, I enjoyed returning home for Christmas, to catch up with my friends at home. Dad drove me back to Southampton on the second Sunday in January, but I wasn't very well, and on the Tuesday the doctor diagnosed chicken pox and ordered me to go home until I had recovered. So I got on a train, despite being highly contagious, and went home, where my mum looked after me and covered me in calamine lotion as required. I spent quite a lot of time 'pink-washed', or so it seemed. After about 10 days, I was well enough to return to Southampton, once more on the train.

I suppose I spent too much time in the next few months focusing on Gary and his requirements. I was helping him with his revision and his dissertation, and didn't spend enough time on my study needs, so much so, that I failed one of my end of year exams. I had to resit it in the September, and luckily I passed that time, otherwise my time at university would have ended prematurely.

Gary had graduated and was offered a job in Furstenfeldbruck, a small town on the outskirts of Munich. My heart sank at this news as it would mean us continuing our relationship at a distance. Looking back, I believe this development enabled me to concentrate on my studies, without too many distractions.

After I had retaken my exam in September, Gary arranged for me to fly to Munich to visit him. During that short break, we visited the famous Oktoberfest and I remember having a fantastic time. The day after we had attended, we heard on the news that a terrorist bomb had exploded at the main entrance on the previous night and 13 people were killed, and hundreds injured. It was very sobering to think that we had been there only a few hours before this occurred. I looked through the photos I had taken at that very spot, a haunting insight into a place where joviality had quickly turned to despair. I had to thank my lucky stars that fate had put us there at a different time.

At the beginning of the second year, I moved into a small end-of-terrace house with two fellow students, Michael and Bronwen. They were a couple, not yet married and, as they were followers of the Mormon religion, they were very well behaved, with separate bedrooms. I believe their approach to life, created a good environment for me to live in. It wasn't the quietest location, the address was on Railway View Road. I was lucky to get the back bedroom so I wasn't continuously seeing passenger and goods trains passing by on the busy track between Southampton and Portsmouth.

The house lacked some of the comfort I had enjoyed in the halls of residence; there was no central heating and the bathroom was in an extra bit that had been built on the ground floor behind the kitchen. Not only did it mean a long journey through the house to reach it, but in the winter months it was freezing in there. There was black mould on the walls caused by inadequate ventilation and insulation, plus ice on the inside of the windows - a situation that wasn't unusual at the time in thousands of homes, but definitely one that filled me with dread when bath time approached!

Staying in touch with Gary was difficult, letters took a long time to arrive, but were always a lovely surprise when they were delivered. The house I lived in didn't have a phone connection, so the only option we had was to arrange a certain time when I would walk to the nearest phone box and wait for him to call me. This was reasonably successful but sometimes frustrating, especially when there was someone already occupying the box when I got there. I used to just hope that he realised what was happening and continued trying until the line was clear. How different it would have been now. I don't think we even contemplated the invention of mobiles and laptops.

At the end of the winter term, Gary bought me a plane ticket and I flew to Munich to spend some time there with him, before his friend drove us back to England just before Christmas. I loved that short break and was able to see Queen play a concert at the Olympic velodrome, a wonderful memory to have.

I split my time between Southampton, Croydon and Munich for the next 12 months. During the summer vacation, I worked for the Home Office in Croydon, in the immigration department. I spent the majority of that time in the post room, processing incoming packages that contained passports and associated documents - it was quite an interesting job for someone with an innate curiosity about other people's lives, especially celebrities.

Of course, I had to sign the Official Secrets Act, so I cannot regale you with any tales.

My studies continued well and, in July 1982, I graduated with a 2:1 and became a Bachelor of Arts. Leading up to this point, I had been carefully considering my career options, which appeared quite limited. Teaching had always been something I wanted to go into, but apparently at that time, the number of children in the population was in decline and teachers weren't in great demand. I was told that if I studied for a one-year PGCE, there was no guarantee a teaching job would be available at the end of it.

I was advised that other opportunities might come in banking, librarianship or retail, so I decided to pursue retail as my career path. I must have written hundreds of letters to every high street retailer, enquiring about head office positions or branch management training schemes. I had a handful of positive responses which led to interviews, but the only company that offered me anything was WH Smith. I wanted to join their Branch Management Training Scheme, which was aimed at graduates, but for some reason they decided I only had the talent to be put on their secondary scheme, which was for department managers.

During the interview process I had spoken a lot about my love of music, so was delighted when I was told that I was to be placed as a trainee Record Department manager in the West London area. This suited me as I was able to return back to live with my parents near Croydon and commute by train every day.

The first store I worked in was located in Putney, where I started to learn the basics about retail and the responsibilities. That Christmas I was placed on the computer and games counter, becoming an 'expert' in handheld game consoles and the newly introduced Sinclair ZX81s and Spectrums. It was an exciting time for new technologies and was a great experience for me personally.

In late 1983, I was reassigned to the Hammersmith branch and gained promotion to Deputy Department manager. This store was a lot bigger and the range that we stocked was much broader, especially when in 1984, we became one of the first shops to offer our customers Compact Discs.

The lady who was my department manager accepted promotion to Deputy Branch manager at another store, so I stepped up to become solely responsible for the management of the department - staff, stock, budgets - all mine. There was a lot of pressure on a day-to-day basis, but keeping my staff in line, ensuring they completed their tasks properly and disciplining them if necessary, was the bit of the job I enjoyed the least.

I was more interested in the mechanics of the stock management. At that time everything was done manually - inventories were done regularly and bestsellers counted every day. There was no computer system working out algorithms for you, the purchasing of stock was based on one's own experience and knowledge - your own gut feeling. It was exciting to make such decisions and then pick up the phone to the record companies' distribution centres and place the orders yourself. It was long-winded without all the automatic online ordering that was introduced later in the decade, but it felt immediate and personal.

At the beginning of 1985, I became aware that WH Smith were moving their head office from central London to a newly built facility in Swindon. There were many members of staff who did not want to relocate, so several positions came up on the internal vacancy lists. I saw this as a great opportunity for myself and applied straight away. After several rounds of interviews, I was offered a job as a junior buyer.

This was so exciting for me and I was to report to my new manager on Monday 3rd June. I had a few days holiday to use, so took them before I was due to start. Unfortunately my world was turned upside down during that interlude, when my dad suffered a major heart attack and was hospitalised in intensive care for over a week. There was no way I could move to Swindon during this episode, my mum needed me and I wanted to be with her. Sadly my dad passed away on 2nd June, the day before I was due in Swindon. The HR department were very understanding and a new start date of 17th June was agreed, as this allowed me enough time to grieve, help mum through her trauma and attend his funeral.

It was a difficult couple of weeks, but on the Sunday (16th), I packed my suitcase and made my way, by train, to Swindon. I was sad that my dad couldn't give me a lift like we had originally planned. My entry into the world of Head Office was even more difficult than anticipated. I was two weeks behind the other new starters, so missed out on the camaraderie that might have been more natural in normal circumstances. Emotionally I was a little bit of a wreck, but I put my brave face on and powered through, not wanting to show any weakness.

For the first few weeks, I was staying in a hotel in Highworth - it needed to be somewhere on a bus route as, at that point, I had a driving licence but no car. This was not the best arrangement for me. The idea of living in a hotel had always appealed to me, but in reality, I felt isolated and very alone. It would have been much better with all the technology available today, but my only means of contact then was the phone box in the market square. I managed to get back to London at the weekends, but I needed to settle down and start to feel I belonged.

Eventually I was able to team up with a couple of other girls in a rental property near to the office. I had my own space at last. After a few months, as part of the relocation package offered by WH Smith, I was able to secure my own 2-bedroom house in Highworth. Looking back this was an incredible moment for me. I would never have taken this bold step if the company hadn't been offering the full service. All I had to do was find a house that was selling for 3 times my annual salary, and they did the rest - arranged the mortgage, did the legal stuff - everything.

The day I got the keys was a real bittersweet moment for me - I imagined how proud my dad would have been of his 'little girl', a homeowner at 24 - unbelievable! The other great thing about the relocation package was the offered mortgage subsidy. Imagine the beauty of only having to pay a fixed 4% interest while WH Smith stumped up the difference for anything over that. This worked out to be a lot as the mortgage rate soared to 14 or more per cent in the late 1980s/early 1990s.

My life as a music buyer was quite a steep learning experience. I was in a world of big business, responsible for buying stock for over 200 branches, which accounted for approximately 20 per cent share of the total UK market, across all retail outlets. I quickly became aware that I was in a privileged and important position. After a few early setbacks, I settled into my stride (which was normally taken in high heels and dressed in a power suit with sizeable shoulder pads, topped off with the obligatory 80s bubble perm).

The record companies would send their sales representatives along to see the buying team on a monthly basis. These men, because they were all men, would present their forthcoming releases and persuade us to support them with large pre-order quantities backed with in-store and external marketing campaigns (the WH Smith name was very well trusted by the buying public).

As a young female in an extremely male dominated industry these were interesting times. I don't think that many of the men who dealt with me initially were used to a young woman making such big decisions. The women in their offices were usually the secretary or the admin staff - 'dolly birds', I suppose. There were occasions when they requested to see someone more senior - more male - if they felt that business wasn't going their way, but in time I gained their respect, and my managers normally backed me all the way. I developed a good understanding of what would sell and what was a non-starter - I really felt that my 'gut feeling' was normally correct.

During this period, technology started to become a big part of the job. Before 1986-7, most data we collected was done manually, branches were telephoned and they gave us sales figures on the top sellers; this was the only way we could gauge our success. Barcodes then started to appear on LP sleeves etc, which was closely followed by a revolutionary EPOS (Electronic Point of Sale) system. Gradually the use of computer data became normal and my role developed to take an even closer control of stock levels and budget parameters.

I guess that the best things about the job were the 'freebies'. I was always being offered amazing opportunities to go to concerts, showbiz parties and other unique events. For some of the record companies, especially the smaller labels, my presence at one of their events was well received, not only by the senior management but sometimes by the artist or group themselves - it was seen as a sign that WH Smith believed in them and their potential - we had influence.

It was easy to overlook the fact that these invites were looked upon by some as bribes, but I like to think that I remained professional (well most of time). Again, there were occasions when the gathered men would 'push their luck' with the young ladies in their company. The odd pat on the bum, the gentle squeeze around the waist was quite normal, and apparently accepted. I don't think that a sexual conquest would have been frowned upon by them - indeed I was made aware later, that bets had been made between them on who would get me into bed first! I must have been so naive, as this didn't ever occur to me at the time.

It is difficult for me to pick out the most memorable events I was lucky enough to attend, but perhaps I could mention a few. Some of you might remember the BPI/BRIT Awards ceremony presented disastrously by Mick Fleetwood and Sam Fox. Well, I was there in the Royal Albert Hall, seated in a loggia box with the members of the group 'The Shadows', as a guest of their record label. It was a big night for their friend and colleague, Cliff Richard, who collected the prestigious Lifetime Achievement award.

The awards ceremony was an absolute shambles and rather embarrassing, to be honest. There were lots of technical errors that could not be corrected as the show was going out live on the BBC. Nevertheless, I had a lovely time sharing a bottle, or two, of bubbly with Bruce Welch and Hank Marvin, who later, at the after-party at the Grosvenor House hotel, introduced me to Cliff as their 'new friend' – priceless!

Another good one was the party at the Waldorf hotel in London, that was held after Madonna had performed at Wembley Stadium. There were lots of celebrities among the attendees, in addition to Madonna herself - most memorable was George Michael.

My friend and colleague Alison loved, even adored, the man. I said to her that she should go up to him and speak to him, but she said that she couldn't do that without someone introducing her to him. Fuelled by a 'little bit' of alcohol, I strolled up to him. I introduced myself and then turned around to Alison and beckoned her over, "This is Alison", I told him, "She is one of your biggest fans and would love to meet you", at which point I left them alone, together. I watched from a short distance away, happy with my handiwork!

I could give accounts of more times : flying to Paris to see Pink Floyd play at the Palace of Versailles, going to the south of France to see the Eurythmics play a concert on the beach at Juan-Les-Pins, attending the George Michael album launch soirée at the Savoy, where the guest list included Elton John and, my teenage idol, David Cassidy (swoon) ... and many, many more.

Just before my 30th birthday, in May 1991, a change was made in the senior management of the WH Smith retail division and you know that old adage - a new broom sweeps clean - well it certainly did. A new approach was introduced and it was decided that I had become too comfortable in my job, and despite the fact that I was excellent at it, and well respected in all areas, I needed to expand my horizons and move over to buying paper clips, photo frames or something else equally uninteresting.

I fought this decision but eventually I decided that the time had come for me to move on. I felt that I needed to get back to London, and I definitely wanted to stay with my special field of expertise. An opportunity came up to join a company that had a huge operation in America, whose ambition it was to crack the European market - the UK was its first target (as we spoke the same language).

This was a complete change in many ways. The scale was so much smaller but the challenges a lot harder. I had come from being a big fish in a smallish pond, and was now an almost invisible minnow. It took me a bit of time to adapt my skills to my new world, but in time, I became a huge asset to the company. My voyage through the 1990s continued my series of amazing experiences - I was very fortunate to be in the right place at the right time.

Oh, I forgot to mention … there was always lots of hard work in between the partying and quite a few headaches and heartbreaks along the way.

Joyce graduating as a teacher in 1949

Jo shopping in London in the 1950s   *Rosemarie bell-ringing*

Maureen at her Hall of Residence Formal (1960)

Jude in 1960 with flatmates Anna and Rosemary

Jocelyn riding a scooter in Greece in the 1980s

Carol with Cliff Richard in 1987

3 WORK AND FAMILY

So now we are all gradually changing our priorities. Most of us have families and are settled into routines. We have experienced death of loved ones and our own families are growing up around us.

The world around us was having its ups and downs. Concorde was getting ready to be retired, Princess Diana died, and we had the gales in the south. Decimalisation was another change; everyone had to learn decimal, especially if working in shops. However, life goes on.

Rosemarie   *1958 to 1972*

These were years of great changes in my life before I settled into the tedious, if not unwelcome, years of being a housewife and mother.

I got engaged before my 22nd birthday. We heard, through WI friends of my mother's, of some land being developed. Never scorn the WI !!!!!!! We bought two plots, planning to put up one house. I had been to the Ideal Home Exhibition with my mother and had seen a bungalow which took my fancy. For years my husband joked that having seen said bungalow I had to find someone who could afford to pay for it and that was why he was accepted by me.

We went to buy the plans and found there was an alternative, similar but a chalet bungalow. We opted for this. Planning permission went through eventually and the build started.

I got married just after my twenty third birthday. Bells were rung before and after the service and hand bells during the reception. It was a gloriously sunny day. My husband had had a stag night. Hen nights were unheard of. Guests did not leave the reception before the bride and groom. We left about 5pm. Guests then left the reception, though partying continued at the home of my parents.

The first night we stayed near Lydd as we had the car booked on an early flight to Le Touquet the following morning. There were regular scheduled flights at that time. We drove through France, Germany and Austria, stopping at various places along the way and ending up at Salzburg during the music festival. We had booked only one event, The Marionette Theatre. There were street parades of bands from local villages. The town was vibrant.

Back home we lived with relatives for a year as the house was not ready. I had always been scornful of people who went on strike. My husband went on strike two weeks after our return from honeymoon. Fortunately it did not last long.

After a year our house-build was finished and we moved in. I got a job near it in the local Junior School. I was there a year, leaving in the July. The baby was due in October. There were rules about how many weeks before a birth one had to give up work and this fitted in neatly. It meant giving up the job completely as there was no such thing as maternity leave.

The consultant at that time warned me that having a negative blood group while my husband's was positive may mean anti-bodies and a 'blue baby' whose blood would have to be changed at birth. In the event this never happened and all was fine. I did have the baby in hospital and was in for ten days which was the norm. By the time I was pregnant with my daughter I had the same warning but medicine had progressed and the baby's blood could be changed while it was still in the womb. Thankfully again all was well and intervention was not needed. There was a shortage of district midwives where I lived and it had to be a hospital birth. I was in for eight days which had become the norm. On both occasions my husband sent me a magnificent bouquet of flowers to the hospital paid for from my housekeeping allowance!

When the first baby was born there was no central heating in the house and the weather turned cold. We left an electric fire on in the bedroom all night. I put the baby in his pram outside on the porch each morning with the encouragement of the health visitor but only for a week or two for on Boxing Day 1962 snow began. It was deep and pushing a pram along the road was not possible. There was snow in the garden for ninety one days. By the time my grandchildren were born the guidance was not to put a baby outside.

My son was a hungry baby and was put on cereal at four weeks (as well as the milk of course). My grandchildren did not get solids until four months at the earliest.

In 1969 I wore tights for the first time under trousers, as opposed to stockings and suspenders.

My husband worked for British Aircraft Corporation in the Flight Test department. It involved working abroad and he went on a seven-week trial leaving me at home with a seven-month-old baby. For the first hour after he left I remember being bothered at the responsibility but rallied quickly and just 'got on with it'. There was no alternative as he loved his job and would not even discuss the possibility of a change of employment.

He had an office in Wisley, on the airfield not the RHS gardens. Later when the Concorde project came on line he had an office in Bristol, Fairford, Wisley and Toulouse. He was often away for weeks at a time. He loved the travel and in later years took me to many of the places to which he had been deployed, possibly one of the most exciting being South Africa and a trip to the Kruger National Park. Few wives went along for trial tours of duty as BAC employees worked long shifts when away. Time abroad meant large investments of money for the company.

During one trial my son ran a high temperature and it seemed would have to be hospitalised but the crisis passed.

Huw started school and I did some supply work. My daughter was born in June 1969. Concorde was to be flight tested at Fairford. Fairford had a ten thousand feet runway suitable for Concorde.

I think it was the norm in those days for wives to go with their husbands. I was not averse to change but I was told rather than consulted that we would leave Farnham and move within travelling distance of Fairford.

I started house hunting. At that time house prices were rising rapidly. It was a sellers' market and properties sold virtually overnight. I viewed houses from Hungerford to Brize Norton to Tetbury. A friend, renting nearby, heard of a house coming on the market in Poulton. It was an executors' sale.

Poulton is not on the flight path for Fairford, an important consideration as the number of flights in and out of Fairford could escalate. We were at the agents at 9am when viewing opened and had put in an offer by 9.30am. The offer was accepted and it became ours in December 1971.

The house needed renovating and I noted that even the loo seats had woodworm. With planning permission in place the house was gutted. One of the alterations was to do away with the baize soundproofed door used by the butler to reach the dining room from the back quarters. We had no butler. There was a complete bell system but that was ripped out, there being no servants to answer the bells! Like many builders before and since, the building company doing the alterations did not run to plan and renovations were still going on when we moved in.

The house had belonged to a Miss Thomas and for years people would say, "Oh, you are living in Miss

Thomas's house". The house in Farnham took three weeks to sell, which was longer than the norm, but it did sell. We moved in April 1972.

Poulton had two shops, with a post office in one, and a pub. There was a garage that sold petrol but also had car repair facilities. There was a Brownie pack and a Cub pack. There was a church choir for boys and girls who were still at school. I was invited to join a group who played bridge regularly, but I declined that offer. There was a WI which I did join. There was a lunch club which met once a month and I went to some of those meetings. There was a Mothers' Union but I did not join that until several years later.

The vicar lived in the village. He was a leading light, hosting sherry parties in the Vicarage for say flower arrangers one week, then Sunday School helpers, sidesmen, readers and so on. Each November he had a big bonfire for children in the village with fireworks contributed by all.

I became a church flower arranger, and for some seven years was church treasurer. I helped with Sunday School on a rota basis. The church yard was kept tidy by volunteers and I sometimes helped my husband there. So Poulton was a vibrant village if one chose to join in all or some of the activities offered.

There were only three bells in Poulton so no change ringing. I went to ring in some local churches but as my husband had become a church warden and Huw was in the choir it meant we did not worship as a family, so I gave up bell ringing and went to church in Poulton.

I was keen to go back to work and got a job in a two-teacher school in a village near Lechlade. At the interview I was quizzed about my family including my intentions with regard to having or not having more children and what I would do if one of my children was ill. These would not be legal questions now. My husband's aunt had retired to Fairford and would look after my children should the need arise.

As it happened my husband was the one who became ill and his aunt came to care for him, an eventuality that those interviewing me for a job had not considered. After seven weeks he returned to work. A tolerant head let me take Penny to work with me. I taught the infants. I was in that school for seven years.

After 1972 we had seaside holidays in North Wales and also went to Spain and Portugal. Narrow boat holidays were a favourite and over time we went on many of the canals in England and Wales. My parents had a caravan at Selsey and we went there some weekends but my husband disliked caravanning. We had a trip to Oberammergau. There were days out including going to see the Tutankhamun exhibition in London.

Christmas recalled.
I asked my children what they recalled about Christmas when they were young, small incidences, not just presents. My son recalled a discussion about wrapping presents, the time no one had bought Sellotape - remember shops closed around 5pm on Christmas Eve. There was no shop attached to the local garage open on Christmas Day, no Tesco open on Boxing Day, no computer to order groceries to be delivered at the housewife's chosen time on Christmas Eve. My daughter remembered getting her first pound note.

My husband's aunt, his grandmother, my parents and an uncle of mine stayed with us over Christmas, a good family time. There were sixpence pieces in the Christmas pudding. The Christmas cake, pudding and mincemeat were home-made. No buying ready-weighed ingredients in Waitrose to make the cake using a TV cook's recipe. There was always a Christmas tree and paper decorations.

Jo   *1970 to 1989*

1970

So we just carried on with our lives. Frank's sister Pauline and her son David moved out and went to the house at Basingstoke Road with Frank's brother Fred and Sheila where there was more room, so we now had, for the first time for about six years, our own space. We still saw a lot of them because David was still at the same school as our two and Pauline was working at Cornhill full-time. With Fred and Sheila's son we still had the four kids with us when it was not school time. It worked OK. They were both saving hard to get their own homes.

1971

We, Frank and I, used to be called upon occasionally to help out at other shops either if someone was poorly or the shop was without a manager for some reason or other! Also in this year I was asked if I would like to work at The Ideal Home Exhibition in London. Of course I was delighted. I went up by train and the company had a stand promoting our shops and the drinks we sold. There were two or three ladies (mostly manager's wives) and a couple of area supervisors. We would also have higher management popping in to show their faces. Well, I got a couple of new minidresses out of that experience!

1972

Decimalisation of course. Everyone had to be competent enough to hold their own with the customers, so each area of about half a dozen shops had little gatherings where we were taught and had tests to make sure we knew what we were doing.

It was good to have some time away from our own shops and meet some of the other managers and wives. We also used to go to various gatherings where we were often introduced to new wines or talks from 'wine masters' about different products. Frank went to a few wine tasting events to help out with serving the wine.

1973

Frank's brother Fred was gradually moving up the property ladder. He and his wife had bought a house in Woodley, a suburb of Reading, then sold again and were eventually living just up the road. Pauline was buying a little house just ten minutes' walk away across the main road.

We used to have great New Year's Eve parties. We would gradually be getting our strength back and could relax after the seasonal rush in the shop.

1974

Our children, Joanna and Martin, were going to the same school at this time. Joanna in the last year of the Juniors passed her Eleven Plus and went to Bulmershe School in Woodley which was then a Grammar School. By the time Martin was eleven it had changed to Comprehensive, so he was able to go to the same school. He had quite a busy social life as well being heavily into the Scouts. He carried that on until more or less the present day (he retired from Scouting as a Cub leader in 2021).

1975

We decided to sell our house, which was now empty, and perhaps buy something on the coast, so we explored as much as we could several areas that were within easy travelling distance of Reading. Our first idea had been the Bogner Regis area, but we were not too keen, so kept looking.

I was learning to drive by then. Friends in the nearest shop to us, about fifteen minutes' drive away, were in the same position, in that Anne also wanted to learn. So Frank went with Anne, and her husband, Graham, taught me. Finally, at the third attempt I passed my test, 29 July 1976 - a red letter day. I now had so much more independence. I got another job, collecting insurance payments for various types of policies, which at that time were collected weekly in cash. As a relief collector I travelled all over Reading, Maidenhead and Henley. At the time we had a large white Ford Zodiac, and dressed to kill in my mini-skirts I enjoyed driving around and exploring all the local areas.

1977
Joanna and Ray married, they honeymooned in our flat, before coming back to their house in Reading.

We gradually got used to being on the coast, or at least near it, whenever possible for a lot of the time. We also went once, for a week, to the Isle of Wight which we could see from our beach. We just popped along to Lymington and caught the ferry.

1978
We finally sold our house. We looked around Reading itself. We saw one which we fancied. It had probably been built just before the war and it really needed doing up, but at that time we were not sure we could manage it. So we looked to the sea-side again and finally found a flat at Highcliffe. It was a beautiful flat, on the third, top, floor. Out of the window one could just about see the sea. There was a small woodland area with a path which led down to the beach. We spent some lovely times there. When more work was carried out on the M3, by-passing Winchester, it was an even better journey.

We used to go down Tuesday night when we had shut the shop at 9.30pm. We would have all day Wednesday then leave early Thursday morning and get back to open the shop at 10am. We also spent our holidays down there and let it out to a few close friends and family.

1981

Some friends, other managers, got a transfer to a branch in Bournemouth, Westcliffe. Another couple transferred to the Canford Cliff shop so it set our minds going. We mentioned to the office that we would be prepared to go south and did not need accommodation if they had a shop that needed a manager.

We knew we wanted to be in that area but could not see ourselves living permanently in a flat, however nice it was, so we started looking around in the area. Bransgore came up, a small village slightly inland. In trade papers we saw a shop with a flat for sale! We made enquiries, viewed it and got to know the owners quite well. However, deep down, it was obvious they were not sure. They pulled out but at least then we had not sold our flat. This had however introduced us to a new area and we liked it. It had the advantages of being ten minutes from the sea but also countryside.

We bought a new house in Bransgore, and had an extension built at the front and we really loved that house. Our back garden was on the farm lane. We worked out that the hedge at the bottom was a couple of hundred years old.

1983

There was finally an offer from the company of a shop to manage. Well two, actually, to choose one from. They were both lock-ups within reasonable reach of our house and the sea. One was at Parley, a nice little shop but on a main road, the other was at West Moors. This was in a growing village and we thought that it showed more promise. It was the right choice - different customers, but we gradually built up the trade and became well known in the village.

However the ride from Bransgore to West Moors, although beautiful, was a bit of a drag. So we put our house on the market and looked for something in the village.

1984

We finally bought a bungalow in West Moors. We found an old one two minutes' walk away but that fell through at the last minute, so we had to start looking again. We found a newer one five minutes from the shop but did not think it so nice at first. However gradually we began to like it. It had a large back garden that disappeared into the woods. The garden was in a terrible state but Frank worked hard on it and it became our pride and joy.

1985

Trade increased, we were doing well. I and the lady that had taken over the West Parley shop organised the next couple of Christmas events for all our local branches, but the company were gradually stopping those. - a shame as we used to enjoy them.

I then decided to change my job. I joined Bournemouth Council in the Engineers' Department and was there for the introduction of the Wheelie Bin replacing the old-style bin collections! I first worked at the refuse bin depot in the office and got to know the bin-men and answered telephone queries about the new system. Then when we had finished introducing the wheelie bins I was moved to Bournemouth Town Hall, still in the Engineers' Department but more to do with local roadworks.

1988

Martin and Alison got married in the October. We provided all the booze whilst the bride's parents paid for the rest. It was a lovely family event. As Alison's father worked for Reading University we were able to have it there, at Whitenights Park. This was near where we used to live in Earley. The happy couple arrived in a horse drawn carriage. They were buying their first house in Reading.

1989

Frank was poorly and decided that he would retire early. The area supervisor took us out to lunch and tried to persuade Frank just to have some time off but Frank was adamant he wanted to retire.

About this time my sister Carole and husband Keith had decided to make a change. They sold their house in Chingford and were ready to move. We had a holiday with them where we travelled around looking in northern university towns - Liverpool, Manchester, Sheffield, Wakefield, ending up in Bolton where we visited Frank's sister Irene.

After much discussion we decided it was a good idea, and that Bolton fitted all our requirements! Carole and Keith moved to Bolton and started buying older terraced houses that were near the college. They moved into one themselves while they got to know the area.

We put our bungalow in West Moors onto the market but were going on holiday so left the keys with an estate agent. We came back and the agent told us that someone had viewed, but they must complete in three weeks or they would pull out. I went back to work at the Council and told them that I was sorry - I couldn't give a month's notice, only three weeks. Carole and Keith told us that they were just in the process of buying a little student house round the corner from theirs – do take it over.

We had two cars at that time – a Ford Mondeo and I had a beautiful little MGB. We decided we would not need two so resold my MGB to the man in the village that we had bought it from. So within three weeks it was all completed and we were moving to Bolton – a huge change in our lifestyle and surroundings.

Maureen   *1968 to 1984*

Eighteen months after the birth of my second baby I took the training offered by the National Childbirth Trust and became an ante-natal teacher myself. This involved day trips to London and the occasional weekend, when I would stay with my sister, Jean. Graham was great at finding interesting things to do with the children, but catering was something of a challenge for him. I would leave a fridge full of easy-cook food for the family. Nevertheless, one weekend I discovered he had instructed Janet to cut the potatoes into chips and parboil them before he deep-fried them!

Together with two other local NCT members we set up the South Dorset Branch, which is still thriving today. Since we only had three members and one did not want to hold an official position, I became Chair and the other lady became Secretary/Treasurer. We expanded steadily with each new class we taught.

One year we decided to raise our profile by entering a float in the Poole Carnival. We chose as a theme The Old Woman Who Lived In A Shoe. The husband of one of our members designed a huge red platform-soled peep-toe shoe with windows, doors and a chimney. It had window boxes with paper flowers in them. It was made of papier mache, on a solid wooden frame which Graham and I constructed in the sweltering evenings of 1976. We sometimes worked until midnight, dressed only in trunks and bathing costume, the minimum required for decency.

We wanted to have our children on board blowing bubbles at the crowd. Safety was not an issue as they could be safely penned inside the shoe. Toilet arrangements had to be made so we sited a potty in the heel and hung a rug over one of the supporting cross beams for privacy. The shoe became quite a feature on our drive that summer.

Just before the Carnival we discovered that there was a low bridge on the route, so Graham hastily designed a hinge system so that the chimney could be lowered to go under the bridge, a procedure which caused some consternation among the watching crowds.

Our house was a on a new estate on sloping heathland overlooking the Wareham valley. It was split-level, which meant that all of the main rooms were on the first floor, with rooms only at the front on the ground floor. The staircase was something of a problem with small children, particularly as the stair gate proved to be more of a hazard than a help.

However, once, when we had a leak in the upstairs bathroom, we were very excited to discover a 'secret room' at the back of the ground floor – very Enid Blyton! It did only have a head height of about five feet so any plans to use it remained mere fancy.

Living upstairs had the advantage that it gave ten minutes warning of approaching showers, enough time to bring the washing in before it got wet. On very clear summer evenings we could see the Old Harry Rocks in Poole harbour and beyond that to the Solent with the QE2 sailing slowly in.

The gardens on the estate were a nightmare for keen gardeners as nothing grew to its full height, even when loads of topsoil had been added. We made no pretence at being gardeners; our garden was full of natural things – yellow, white and red/yellow broom, prolific blackberry bushes, slow worms, sand wasps and even a nest of baby adders.

Graham made a huge sandpit by digging out a sandy slope and moving the sand to level ground. It was large enough to accommodate six or more children, all digging furiously to try to get to Australia!

We did make one attempt to establish a lawn. I built a retaining wall and levelled off an area using the best of the earth, then we laid down turf – at the beginning of summer 1976 when a hosepipe ban was in place for months. Despite using all the waste water we could, we watched in frustration as the expensive turf died.

The childhood years were not always easy, but I found it particularly hard when my oldest child started school. I felt I was not deemed good enough to educate her any more. In my head I knew it was silly, but I could not easily shake off the feeling.

As the second child approached the same stage he was so ready for school that I established morning 'school' at home. I gave him things to do that would prepare him for lessons - drawing, cutting out, tracing etc. - which he did sitting at his 'desk'. After this he would have his 'milk' (actually his usual Ribena) and then watch a television programme for schools. He loved it and we kept it up for several months up until the summer holidays.

Graham was working long hours in the Road Traffic Division of Plessey, based in Poole. He was part of the West London Experiment, a limited area road traffic control system designed to see whether traffic flows could be improved by linking lights together under computer control. Following this he was made Project Leader for the world's first city-wide traffic control system in Leicester. The long hours left me feeling quite lonely at times.

The seventies brought the oil crisis, high inflation and a series of strikes resulting in the three-day week and television closing down at ten o'clock in the evening. We managed the power cuts pretty well. The children particularly enjoyed going to bed by candlelight. There was no radio or record player when the cuts were on, but our pianola came into its own. Driven by pedalling, this instrument gave us music whenever we wanted.

Heating was trickier. Hot water could circulate using gravity, providing warmth to the upper storey where our main rooms were but it depended on an electrical switch on the boiler. Graham rigged up a big torch battery to give just enough power to operate the switch, so we were not even deprived of heating!

When my daughter was old enough to go to Sunday School I volunteered to help and was promptly asked to start a creche; that began many years of work given to children in church. Graham also began to work in the church with a group of young teenagers, memorably taking them to London in a minibus to see 'Jesus Christ Superstar'.

Our minister identified a number of young couples who were missing the late-night student sessions when we would put the world to rights. The subsequent group became known as the 'Mind Benders', discussing all matters religious or ethical. It was a lifeline for thinking adults in a world that seemed alarmingly superficial and increasingly dominated by advertising.

By the end of this period money had become tight and I started looking round for a job. There was very little part-time work and it was all low-grade stuff. I eventually got a post on the shop floor of a furniture company. It was not a success, as I refused to play what I called the numbers game, and the trade was in the doldrums anyway. I was very glad to leave when we moved to Fairford after Graham began working for Ticket Equipment in Cirencester.

In 1984 we moved into our house on a cold wet day in February after an overnight stay in a boarding house in Cirencester. As soon as we arrived we were welcomed by neighbours – two with cakes and another with coal for the open fire as we could not get the oil-fired boiler to work.

On our very first night we had a visitor to stay, the minister from our church in Broadstone, who was on his way to a conference. It was quite a rush to get beds sorted and curtains up in time for his arrival, especially after all the neighbourly interruptions.

A week later our neighbours invited us to a party at their house and introduced us to all the members of FADS (Fairford Amateur Dramatic Society).

A few weeks after we moved in I saw a notice in the newsagent's window, calling for volunteers to take part in a Son et Lumiere to be put on in the church in September. I suggested to the family that it would be a good way to meet people and to find out about the history of the town at the same time. The project had been intended as an event to celebrate the Queen's Silver Jubilee the previous year but had not been ready in time. In fact the script was still being written as we proceeded with rehearsals.

Graham was happiest behind the scenes. He became the sound effects man, taping many from BBC records which he bought. Some songs he recorded live then edited to fit. One day he incessantly played the Boer War song 'Boots, boots, boots, boots, tramping over Africa' trying to get the timing precisely right; the rest of us were sick of the song by the end of the day! More challenging still was the manufacturing of the sound of a cannon ball hitting the church. But the effect he was most proud of was the sound of Concorde starting at the back of the church and flying over people's heads, making them duck.

There were over seventy actors involved, many taking two or three parts. I was in turn a mediaeval lady (in a dress that looked fabulous but was actually hanging in tatters), a devout Protestant lady at prayer, and a young woman reading a soldier's letter home during the First World War. The children appeared at various times through the ages. Even Graham was persuaded to play a courtier to Henry VIII. Undoubted stars of the show were two live Cotswold sheep, one of which was very happy to go on stage and very reluctant to leave it.

The church was packed for a whole week but with a quarter of the town involved in some way or other nothing else happened that week. Apart, that is, from the death of Edward Keble, retired vicar of Fairford and descendant of John Keble, the priest/poet. It had taken 24 hours to set up all the sound and lighting equipment; there was no way it could be removed for a funeral. Fortunately the vicar declared that such an important funeral would take much longer to arrange and we were all able to breathe again.

Graham and I were particularly touched by a speech on the last night recognising that now there were no longer Old and New Fairfordians, just Fairfordians; we felt we belonged already.

Graham had a job as Chief Engineer on a project to develop a microprocessor-based ticketing machine for buses. It was very stressful and the company went through several owners in the five years of the project but in the end it was extremely successful. Oxford was the first city to use the machines and we were astonished to find them still in use on park-and-ride buses 16 years later. Apparently the drivers had thrown out the replacements and demanded their Timtronics back again!

I did not get back into computing until 1980. Having a young family I wanted only part-time work and that was almost unheard of in programming. After moving to Fairford I found a small company in Cirencester who were willing to take me on part-time and allow me to work from home sometimes.

I was working on another state-of-the-art machine, the Cado, which had yet another Assembler language and wanted its programs in tiny chunks of just 240 bytes. That was quite a challenge. Coding had to be really efficient and use the minimum number of instructions to complete the task.

After a year or two, Apple brought out its first microcomputer and I was transferred onto programming that. There were technical problems with the new hardware, and I managed to blow up the one and only machine, which wiped out all the profit from the contract. Not my finest hour!

When the firm got into financial difficulties, I was made redundant, and shortly afterwards it went into liquidation.

I found work as a contractor for a firm in Swindon who were producing microprocessors. Like many other British computer manufacturers they were unable to compete with the American giants and went into liquidation after I had been with them only six months.

In 1983 Graham left Ticket Equipment and, with an initial contract from them, he and I set up our own computer consultancy. It was something he had always wanted to try and it came at the right time for me. It was all very exciting, furnishing a spare room, buying our very own microprocessor and working on software development together.

What we had not really taken into account was the amount of time the admin would take, a distraction that always came at the bottom of the list of things to do. Also, Graham was a perfectionist, so he was never satisfied that software was good enough to be delivered to the customer. We did try to engage someone to join us but in reality we could never afford another salary. Eventually the stress overcame Graham and I had to look for a full-time job.

Jude   *1973 to 1982*

In late August 1973 I went with a long-term boyfriend to Crete on one of those package holidays that were then all the rage. On the plane to Athens (Crete not yet having its own international airport) a couple of likely lads were sitting in the seats in front of us We met them again in the queue for passport control and later at the welcome drinks party at the hotel. Gareth and Geoffrey were both Cambridge law graduates and had only the day before attended the wedding of another of their Cambridge contemporaries (Richard and Zo) who were honeymooning for the first week in Athens and the second, by co-incidence, in Crete.

The four of us immediately got on like a house on fire and spent the entire holiday in each other's company, hiring a car and exploring the island together. Gareth had been the only one of us to have had the foresight to bring with him his International Driving Licence so only he could drive. He was a dreadful driver and there were some terrifying moments going over the mountains on narrow unguarded tracks beside precipitous ravines. Gareth would take his eyes off the road and turn round in his seat to talk to us until we screamed at him.

One day Geoffrey decided to have a day on his own at some remote beach on the North of the island and we dropped him and a pile of books off there before the three of us headed off again to explore the South.

It was very late and pitch dark when we got back to the hotel. The three of us had a late supper. Gareth went to find Geoffrey in the room they were sharing but he wasn't there. We all wondered what had happened to him. Several hours later one of us remembered we had dropped him off at that remote beach whose precise location none of us could remember. How could we have forgotten?

We decided that, even though it was well past midnight, we had to get in the car and try to find him. The unmade-up roads were unlit and dangerous. We spent quite a few nerve-wracking hours trying to find where we had dumped him for the day. The beach, when we eventually found it, was silent and dark, the only sound being the waves of the sea gently lapping the shore. We called out for him, but there was no reply.

There was a fisherman's shack at the far end of the beach which had a flickering light from a candle showing under the door. We approached it with some trepidation, but just then the door opened and a fisherman and his wife came out gesticulating and talking wildly in local Greek dialect. They had found Geoffrey after dark on the beach, cold, hungry and upset. They had taken him in, shared their humble supper of fried red mullet with him and laid him to rest on a make-shift bed on the floor of their primitive home, where he was now snoring noisily. We were profuse in our thanks to the fisherman and his wife. It was the small wee hours when we got back with him to the hotel.

The honeymoon couple arrived in Crete and came over to our hotel to visit us. Once again there was an instant rapport, to such an extent that Zo (her nickname) decided to throw a party when they got back to London and to invite us all They were living in a small cottage in Harrow which they decided was far too small for the size of party they wanted, so Richard asked to borrow the spacious Maida Vale flat (it occupied three floors) he had previously been sharing with flat mates.

I had been asked to provide the music and I spent a long time recording all my 1960s records on to a huge reel to reel tape recorder.

On the morning of the party, I awoke with severe abdominal pains and could hardly walk. I almost cried off attending but since everyone was relying on me for the music I made an heroic effort to get to Maida Vale from Caterham (where I was living) to set it up. I asked long term boyfriend to drive me there with all the music paraphernalia.

The party was a good one. Despite the pain, I managed to dance all night with the chap in whose flat it was being held until, doubled up, I came to the conclusion I was ill and needed medical attention. The boyfriend took me to St Georges at Hyde Park Corner where they would have performed an appendectomy had I not already had my appendix removed. Somewhat perplexed they kept me in for the night for observation. The next morning the pain had completely disappeared and no-one to this day knows what had caused it.

Zo and Richard owned a holiday cottage in Devizes and from then onwards we would regularly go down there for weekend parties.

The chap in whose flat the party had been held was also a frequent visitor. I assumed he was a merchant banker or something in the City. I was working in Chancery Lane at the time and quite often would bump into him at some eating establishment in the vicinity during the lunch hour. He usually did not seem to recognise me or if he did, would only nod in acknowledgement and move on. He was a man of few words.

In the Spring of 1974, once the season had opened, he organised a group outing to Glyndebourne. Caterham was on the way and he offered to give me a lift in his then brand new MG. On the way back, I invited him in for a coffee which he accepted, but stayed only to drink it before heading back to Maida Vale. To this day, I shall never know why, but that day I decided to move back to London, knowing (despite no encouragement whatsoever having been given on his part) that there was probably more to this than met the eye. I moved into a flat share with two girlfriends in Maida Hill. Even more remarkable was the fact that at more or less the same time, unknown to me and for reasons even now he cannot explain, he went over to Berlin to end the relationship with his German fiancée, whom he was due to marry in the not too distant future.

In May 1974 he took me to the May Ball at Trinity, his old Oxford college, where I met his younger brother who was still up reading Medicine. At the end of the ball, in the early hours we were unable to retrieve our coats which were in a locked room so, undeterred, he broke down the oak door to get in. He was later fined a heavy whack for the damage caused.

Over the next year he took me out to dinner, the theatre and concerts and introduced me to his parents who were now farming in Lee, a village near Malmesbury. I was now over 30 and feeling the edge of the shelf. I said to his brother that unless something happened pretty soon, I was moving on.

Shortly afterwards, he took me out for dinner and we sat at a table just under a very noisy air-conditioning unit. I was unable to hear a thing. He mumbled something and I said, "What? Sorry couldn't hear you!"

He mumbled again and I couldn't make out what he was saying. "Oh don't bother to talk to me" I said, "I can't hear a word."

He arranged to change tables and at the third try on his part I realised he had proposed. Of course I accepted.

We were formally engaged in December 1975 and married on 20th March 1976 at the Chapel at Trinity College, Oxford. My ex-stepmother's new husband gave me away. I had woken up on the morning of the wedding with a temperature of 104 and can scarcely remember a thing about it, except that it was an exceptionally warm spring day. This was of course the year of the long hot summer. We honeymooned in East Africa. I was now 32.

It was July 1981. I was 37 years old and pregnant with my second child (sex unknown). I was 42 weeks 'gone'. I had put on 5 stone, was huge and unable to move much.

My consultant obstetrician was due to go on holiday on Friday 3rd July. I persuaded him to induce me before he departed. That was memorably painful as I recall.

I was in a London teaching hospital. They wheeled me down to a basement, to a lecture theatre packed with medical students. I was surrounded by a 12 strong team of masked and gowned medics, talking together in hushed voices. It was a long procedure requiring forceps but eventually the baby, a girl, was yanked out, briefly shown to me - she was extremely blue - and whisked away to be resuscitated.

The consultant took off his gown and, flinging his coat around his shoulders, rushed off to catch a plane. Everyone left. I was wheeled on a trolley to a recovery room, and everything went very quiet. The whole basement had emptied. It was, after all, 9.00pm on a Friday night.

I dozed off and when I awoke it was 10.45pm. The lights had been dimmed. There was complete silence. I started shouting "Hallo! Hallo! Is anyone there?"

I did this for a few minutes and then a rough voice answered back, "It's no good you hollering like that, Missus. I'm going to lock up now".

I heard a jangle of keys and locks being turned, and the lights were dimmed even further.

"They'll be down for you in a minute, Luv, not to worry. I'll be glad to get off duty".

So saying, the owner of the voice, with a banging and crashing of doors, vanished.

No-one came to collect me. The trolley must have been at maximum height, but I knew I had to get off it somehow. I jumped and made it to the floor, my legs buckling beneath me. The hospital gown I was wearing fell off. It was too small and the ties at the back were non-existent.

Machines whirred and red and green lights blinked as I tried to find a door. Like a blind person, I groped my way in the dark along corridors, past operating theatres, laboratories and other rooms until eventually I found myself in front of a lift. I pressed the button and could hear it clanging its way down. The doors opened and there inside, looking surprised, were a couple of white coated consultants deep in conversation, who had clearly expected to get out on the ground floor.

I apologised for bringing them down, and clutching the useless gown around me, asked them if they knew on which floor was the maternity ward. "You see", I said, "I have just had a baby and don't know where it is. I need to find it".

They exchanged looks with each other before telling me it was on the 4th floor. They got out on the ground floor and I carried on up to the 4th. I found my way to a ward and an office with nurses in it.

"Hallo", I said hopefully "Do you happen to have a spare baby lying about? You see I've just had one and don't know where it is".

The nurses looked at me strangely and then at each other before saying that I needed the 3rd floor for maternity as this was the psychiatric ward. Any spare babies would probably be on the 3rd floor not on the 4th.

I walked down a staircase to the floor below, holding the gown up in front of me, knowing, and not caring, that my backside was exposed. Finding the baby was my overriding concern.

On the 3rd floor there was, again, a room full of nurses. They were busy, and not wishing to disturb them I sat on a plastic chair and waited. Eventually, one of them, a senior nurse and probably the Matron, looked up and asked if she could help me. I repeated my request. She looked horrified. "I don't think you belong here" she said angrily. "Where have you come from?"

I told her I had been sent down to the 3rd floor from the 4th floor. "And that's where you are going back to my girl" she said.

She seized me roughly by the arm and frogmarched me up the same stairs again to the 4th floor where, in a raised voice, she told the nursing staff there that they should look after their patients, before flouncing off in high dudgeon. She did not hear them calling after her that I was not one of their patients and that they didn't know from where I had come. I was left standing there.

Trying again, I crept back down the staircase to the 3rd floor once more.

"Oh, my giddy aunt!" the senior nurse screeched. "It's not you again, is it? I thought I'd got rid of you".

"Maybe the baby is dead, and you don't want to tell me?" I asked forlornly.

She turned to address the other nurses in the room. "I don't know what we've done to deserve this intrusion" she said. "This woman is looking for a spare baby and keeps escaping from the floor above. Can one of you take her back up there again? I'm going to file a complaint".

At this, a very junior nurse piped up. "Actually", she said, "there IS a spare baby in the end room, and we've been trying to find its mother for hours".

I was led to the end room and there was a baby with a tag around its wrist saying 'Baby X' so I knew it was mine. At the end of the cot was a card saying what time she had been born and her weight. She had been 10lbs 4 oz.

Later that night, feeling unwell, I pulled the cord above my bed to summon a nurse. The cord came off in my hand. I climbed out of bed and found my way to the loo where I promptly collapsed on the floor having 'given birth' to a 9lb placenta which they had failed to remove properly. I dread to think what would have happened if that had occurred whilst I was on my own in the basement a few hours earlier.

Although a 10lb 4oz baby was not a record for the hospital, that AND a 9lb placenta WAS a record. There was a full enquiry held afterwards and I received an abject apology. All they were concerned about was the placenta not having been removed when it should have been. They never knew that I had spent hours unattended in the basement.

It was Tuesday 20th July 1982. Sophie was four and a half and Camilla had just had her first birthday earlier in the month. We were flying the next day to Skiathos for 10 days or so. The cost of a midweek flight had been a bargain. I had finished the packing. It was a glorious hot day with clear blue skies.

My husband had gone into the office for the day in the MG. The only other car we had at the time was a small second-hand bronze coloured Peugeot which we called the tin can.

It was such a beautiful day, I decided the children and I just had to go somewhere and make the most of it. For reasons I can never now explain I came up with the bizarre idea that we should go to Regent's Park, a seven minutes' drive away, and have a picnic near the bandstand. There was music every day during the summer there and I have never before or since gone and listened to a military band playing in a London or any park.

I went into the kitchen and made a child-friendly picnic, grabbed some toys, a small deckchair and a picnic rug, packed the car with it all and strapped the children into their car seats. I started the car, or tried to. It just made an "er er er er er" noise. After 20 minutes of trying to start the car without success, I gave up. I unpacked everything including the children and we had an early lunch (actually more like elevenses) eating the picnic sitting on our back lawn. I periodically went out to try and start the car again, without success. We needed the car to get to the airport the next day and I wondered if I should call out the RAC.

It was only 12.30 and frustrated at being so trapped without transport I then decided we would go for a walk locally. A new delicatessen had opened up just down the road, and for something to do and to get out of the house I put Camilla in her pushchair and the girls and I set off to get something for tea from the new shop.

As we were walking down the road. Sophie said to me: "Mummy! Why didn't you bring your umbrella?"

"What an earth for?" I asked her. "It's a wonderful day, darling, with not a cloud in sight. Why should we have an umbrella?"

"Because it is going to rain and we shall all get very wet".

"I don't think it's going to rain, darling!" I said.

She appeared to be very agitated. "Yes it is! Can't you hear the thunder?"

I looked up at the sky. Yes, I did hear a sort of rumbling noise a distance away but it did not really sound like thunder. I managed to placate her and we proceeded to the new delicatessen. It did not rain either on the way there or back. I tried starting the car again. The ignition would not catch. It was a dead car.

My husband came home round about 5.30pm. I told him we had a problem with the car. He started it first time and wondered why I had had any trouble starting it.

On the six o'clock news that evening we learned about the IRA bomb going off under the Regent's Park bandstand just before 1.00pm - the precise time I and the children would have been sitting right in front of it on our rug and eating our picnic lunch. The 'thunder' Sophie had heard was of course the exploding bombs. To this day, I wonder if we had a guardian angel preventing us from being there.

Jocelyn   *1993 to 2005*

During these years the children grew, as they do, while I continued to teach computing in the Sixth-Form College. However, the subject of psychology soon became very popular and, since I had half a degree in it, I was asked to swap specialisms. In 1993 this allowed me to apply for the job of Head of Psychology at a school in Bristol where Rod could also find work (as a nurse tutor in nearby Bath) which was a good move for both of us.

Bristol was and is an entertaining place to live; we learned to juggle and attended many local festivals. A highlight one year was free entry to Glastonbury festival as Rod was participating in the fire show.

Working as a teacher had the big advantage that, while there was plenty of planning to be done during school holidays, I did not have to attend the school itself and could look after the children at home.

With the old camper-van having gasped its last we looked for a different way to holiday and discovered Euro-camp – tents that were pre-erected on French or Dutch campsites near beaches and even had fridges. Moving around the continent had just become easier with the launch of the European single market and I have many happy memories of our fortnight-long summer holidays, each taken at two or three different Eurocamp sites, with well-appointed playgrounds where children of different backgrounds and languages happily played together.

We all learned to love French food, indeed when my son was admitted for an operation to insert grommets to improve his hearing before starting school and was asked for his favourite food, the nurses, expecting to be asked to supply ice-cream, were startled by his request for langoustines.

Everyday cooking at home was much more basic and relied on a weekly trip to the out-of-town supermarket where parking with small children in the car was easy. The, by now elderly, fridge-freezer was a godsend, keeping mince, bacon and sausages fresh for me to quickly rustle up rice or pasta dishes at the end of the day and cod in batter, chicken kiev, fish fingers or chicken goujons frozen for Rod to heat through when it was his turn to cook.

As the nineties went on, at the children's behest, we became pet owners, first a gerbil or was it two? (I only remember the vet's bill which was five times the cost of the animal itself) and then two rabbits. Rod and I each managed to carve out a little time for ourselves. He went back to university to complete the degree programme in nursing and I socialised with workmates (Friday evenings at the pub after school were sacrosanct) and friends, those made locally through meeting up on the school run or after school children's activities, and those from the towns we had left.

We had purchased a home PC and, with a dial up modem, both Rod and I became active early adopters on the Internet using different versions of chat and email to keep in touch.

In early 1996 I had two small children in Primary School in Bristol and was myself working as a teacher, teaching science, in its overloaded early National Curriculum version, across the lower school and psychology A level to the sixth form.

One fateful day in March, everyone was in the staff room, it was in the days when you still had time to get there from the science block and back during break, when, highly unusually, a silence swept the room. We were all stunned to hear of the Dunblane Massacre; children and their teacher in a Primary School in Scotland had been shot dead by an intruder. The very idea that someone somewhere would take a gun into a school had previously been inconceivable – well apart from the odd air gun that the physics department would borrow for experiments on velocity and momentum.

When you had a minute to yourself, the Times Educational Supplement was required reading for everyone in the profession and, later that year, I spotted what looked to be an ideal job for someone like me, one who was more of a Jack of all trades than a subject specialist. It involved working in science teacher training and research at Loughborough University as well as teaching computing and psychology to sports science undergraduates.

I was fortunate enough to succeed at the interview and, in September 1996, I and the children moved to a village in Leicestershire. My husband stayed with my parents for a few months until he too got a job teaching nearby, teaching nursing that is, at a university in the Midlands.

We settled happily into village life. Working at university meant we could choose when to work from home and our single PC was well used by the whole family, indeed we were among the first to have MySpace profiles and our own family website.

May 1997 was the one and only time that I stayed up all night to watch a British General Election. From the moment Michael Portillo lost his seat we were hooked and Tony Blair's win signalled the first full scale change of government that I remember.

Work too moved fast and the next year I was moved from science education to setting up my own teacher training programme in IT and computing. I became involved in educational research, investigating how best to use different new technologies in teaching and various national initiatives such as the New Opportunities Fund's (NOF) ICT training scheme for all teachers.

At home we had opted for an allotment, as our garden was small, and weekends were often spent weeding or digging. We did our best to eat the results and, with a little experimentation I learned to cook puddings such as apple and blackberry crumble and strawberry fool; vegetables (apart from courgettes which were prolific and indestructible) were more hit and miss.

That August I came back from the allotment for lunch one Sunday to learn that Princess Diana had been killed in a car crash as she fled from paparazzi photographers. Again I was shocked rigid to learn how badly things can go wrong. We had a television at home and regularly watched the news but felt that the 24/7 coverage being given to her unfortunate death was over the top and were not tempted to watch her funeral. With two children under ten we were pretty much occupied full-time anyway.

For holidays we continued to camp near beaches, in a, now bigger, family tent in Devon or Cornwall and revisiting our favourite Eurocamp sites in Brittany and the Vendée. It was just after one such holiday, camping with friends at Treyarnon Bay in the summer of 1998, that I was surprised to discover I was pregnant again. Apparently it wasn't the board used for the surfing lessons we'd splashed out on that were making my breasts uncomfortable after all.

This time around I was lucky to be working at an established University which allowed me full pay for the standard maternity leave of that time, I think it was seven months and, on my return our latest daughter spent a lot of time strapped to my front at work or with a part-time nanny. This was a young lass, a trained nanny, who was out of work with her own newborn, who had been told by her mother to approach us for a job. It's amazing how much, in a small village, everyone looks out for each other. With newborn twins next door but one, we were soon privy to the ins and outs of the local nanny mafia.

As the year 2000 approached my experience in computing made me aware that the Millennium Bug was a very real possibility, however I forgot it long enough to spend New Year's Eve with friends who lived a short train ride from London. We watched the South Bank Millennium celebration fireworks from a spot on Whitehall near Downing Street; the crowds were so dense we couldn't get any closer to the river.

The Millennium Bug proved to be a damp squib and life moved on apace. We welcomed our fourth child, another daughter, in summer 2001 and I spent a lot of time outside with the neighbours watching the small children play in the front gardens. I probably should have said earlier that we lived at the end of a cul-de-sac. There was plenty of green space and zero traffic.

We were outside after lunch one warm Tuesday in September, the toddler was running around with the twins, all of them having first helped dress up the baby, who was now sitting crossly in her bouncy chair in a white fluffy Babygro and a matching fluffy beret, when the twins' father came running out. A plane had just flown into the World Trade Centre, the party broke up and each family went inside to watch on TV. In stunned disbelief I saw the towers collapse in real-time and, yet again, wondered what the world was coming to.

That year I went back after maternity leave to a different department, for the university management had taken issue with Ofsted's intense oversight of education. They had downsized our programmes, the Department of Education was no longer a separate entity and I was redeployed in the Department of Information Science. I actually enjoyed working there; I learned a lot more about web design and picked up several research projects on the uses of technology in teaching.

The children continued to grow, I learned to manage two trolleys on the weekly shop and we acquired two cats and a second family computer. Also, benefiting from subsidised adult education classes that sadly no longer exist, I took up the opportunity to study pastel painting as a hobby.

In 2003 there was another big change, not so much the UK and US invasion of Iraq, which seemed to me to be a done deal, for I had lost interest in national politics, but another job move, this time back into education. I took up the opportunity of a senior lectureship at the University of Bristol and the responsibility for Physics in their science teacher training programme. Rod returned to nurse training in Bath and Swindon, a post now managed by the University of the West of England, Bristol.

My research interests in using new technologies to teach science burgeoned, the older two children were soon onto GSCEs then A levels and we became a four-computer household.

We had again chosen to live in a village outside the city centre, chosen by its proximity to 'good' schools for the four children plus its ease of access to the universities in the city. We quickly found a child minder for the younger two who went, with the minder's own children, to pre-school playgroup and then the village school itself. We were to stay there for sixteen years, the longest I have ever lived in one place.

Rod and I continued to share parenting. It helped that, as university lecturers responsible for supervising students on placement, we were both largely responsible for our own scheduling and one or the other one was often available when the usual childhood accidents and illnesses meant that one of us had to stay home.

Using the Internet was essential for keeping in touch with students, everyday administration and the data processing and writing up necessary to publish research. We both became quite expert. That said, neither of us could quite get our heads around the rules of the many and varied computer games our older two children played.

In 2004 Facebook was launched, My-Space, Bebo and Club Penguin fell out of favour and soon we all had Facebook profiles. Thanks to teacher development funding we also had access to a number of early smartphones that I was researching uses for.

Sadly though, at Christmas, yet another disaster unfolded on TV, the most costly one yet – the Boxing Day Tsunami which sent shock waves across more than one continent. Everyone knew someone who knew someone who was on holiday in Thailand at the time. However, for someone like myself, keen to ensure that we learn to look after our environment, this was soon followed by a note of hope for, in February 2005, the Kyoto Protocol came into force to control climate change.

Carol   *2000 to 2002*

2001 - the year that changed my life – or should that be
– the year that I changed my life?

31st December 2000

My memories of that evening aren't very clear, but
based on the normal way I 'celebrated' New Year's Eve, I
would have been at my sister's house partaking in a party.

It was a tradition started a few years before, by her and
her husband. They gathered their friends and the children
of those friends to indulge in an evening of music, dancing
and drinking. The problem I had with this was that it was a
family commitment I felt compelled to attend, the people
there were their friends, not mine, but we are a family built
on traditions.

When her husband left her in 1996, I assumed that
these parties would be cancelled, but NO, my sister
insisted that he wasn't going to spoil that frivolity by his
absence, and the get-togethers continued. I was unhappy. I
was approaching my 40th birthday. I was alone watching
people who all had life partners and offspring to be proud
of, but I had nothing. Oh, I owned my own house and to
everyone else, I was successful, but I didn't share their
opinion.

I have to rewind about 5 months, back to July 2000. I
was working for a music distribution company as a 'Digital
Fulfilment Manager', a fancy title for a pretty mundane job.
At this stage I had worked in music retail for 18 years and
was quite comfy in that world. I was responsible for
populating the online entertainment stores for some big
household names, such as Tesco and Capital Radio.

One day, out of the blue, I received a phone call from an agency who had been given my name, recommended by one of my clients, for a position that had come up at One-2-One, the mobile phone company, for a Marketing Manager. Looking back I am not sure whether it was the flattery that turned my head, or the promise of a 50% pay increase, but I took the leap and changed jobs, and careers. I didn't really understand how I had got the position. I attended a couple of interviews where I performed badly, but I decided to grasp the opportunity to move on and try something new.

I knew I had made a serious mistake on the first day in my new job. An afternoon spent in a dark room being bombarded with PowerPoint presentations about brand values, marketing speak and corporate babble, convinced me that this world was very different to the slightly irreverent one I had left – but I had made my bed and had to lie in it – lie being an appropriate word.

Every day I entered that office feeling like a fraud. I had no real knowledge of the job I was doing. My colleagues had all studied marketing and had qualifications for it. Sometimes it was as if they were speaking in a foreign language, but I played the game and got on with it. I couldn't walk out as I had a mortgage to pay and a cat to feed!

Another major downside of the job was that it was in offices to the north of London, in Borehamwood, and I lived in south London, so every day I faced over 3 and a half hours on buses, trains and tubes, slogging from one side of the capital to the other. It was a drag, an absolute bore, a complete waste of time. It wouldn't have been so bad if, once I had reached the office, I had an exciting and full day of work to get on with. I couldn't tell anyone though, I had to pretend.

I was feeling pretty desperate as the first months of 2001 progressed. My journeys to and from work were being done in the dark and my life was going nowhere. The people at work would go out to the pub after work, but I had so little in common with them and had such a long commute, that I always rejected the invites. I hadn't had a man in my life for years and I was starting to think I would never find that happiness.

I needed to do something to turn my life around and I made a promise to myself that 'Life would begin at 40'.

My first port of call was the new and interesting world of internet dating. It seemed the only way that a single woman, living on her own, could meet potential partners. I had my reservations about the process, but I decided it was now or never … and so it started.

The old adage that you have to kiss a few frogs before you find your prince, played out in my experience. I had hoped to have a man on my arm when I attended my own 40th birthday party in May, but that wasn't to be. The initial meetings were always a drink in a local pub and a polite thank you at the end of the evening.

The fifth man I met showed enormous potential and we met up a few times in London. However that changed when he admitted that, although he wasn't married, he did live with a woman, who was the mother of his children – binned!

My 40th birthday party was very interesting. I assembled a collection of people from the various phases of my life. In addition to some immediate family, I had colleagues, clients and suppliers from my jobs since I was 24. Sixteen years of 'friends' who had dipped in and out of my life. Perhaps unfairly, I perceived that the majority of the 50 or so people in the room, were strangers to me. The alcohol consumed made me feel quite melancholy about the transient nature of friendships and loyalty.

Exactly one month after my birthday, on a Saturday morning in June, HE appeared on my computer screen – MY prince! It turned out to be a whirlwind romance. We met, we got on, we enjoyed each other's company – it was perfect.

At the end of August, we had our first long weekend away together – I took him to a hotel in Cirencester and showed him all the places in the area that had been special to me in the past, when I was happy. Based on the fact that we enjoyed the weekend together we quickly organised a trip to Greece for the middle of September, flights to Athens booked for 16th September.

Tuesday 11th September 2001
Another boring day in the office, only bearable because in the evening I was meeting up with Ian and some of his work colleagues in central London for a session of Ten Pin bowling.

As usual, my team had all been to lunch in the canteen and wandered back into the office just before 2p.m. Everyone's first instinct was to check their work emails, but mine was to quickly scan the news headlines. 'Plane hits tower of World Trade centre in New York'.

I read it but it made no immediate impact on me. My thoughts were that it was probably just a tourist trip gone wrong, I had heard that they did such excursions over the Manhattan skyline. My phone rang, it was Ian.

"Have you read about what's happening in New York?" he sounded excited. "About the plane? Yeah I just saw that", I replied. "Jesus, it's a catastrophe … there must be hundreds dead".

I didn't understand what he was talking about, how could a small 6 seater plane, because that was what it was in my head, cause a catastrophe?

Suddenly the peace of the office was shattered. One of our copy writers was exclaiming "What the f***?", at the top of his voice.

"I'd better go", I said to Ian, "I'll call you later", and I put the phone down. "Have you seen this stuff in New York?", the office was buzzing now. "What an awful accident" were the first comments heard.

Everyone was busily reviewing the news sites. There were pictures coming online by now and I could see what Ian had meant. Frank, the copy writer, had only just returned from New York so he had a clearer image in his head of the vastness of the situation.

"Another one's gone into the other tower now – it's no accident, this is deliberate". "Oh those poor people".

Sitting in a glass-enclosed office tower block, I suddenly thought not only of the people on the plane, but of all the people who had been doing exactly what I was doing at that moment, sitting at their office desk quietly surveying the web. The impact, the speed, the fuel, the fire, the horror.

My boss' head suddenly appeared over my workstation divider. Someone had switched some TVs on in the meeting rooms, "You might want to go and see the live coverage on BBC news", she suggested.

There was one member of the team who was starting to panic. She was on her mobile immediately trying to get through to someone. Her face was etched with fear.

"What's the matter with Sejal?" I asked. "It's her sister, she lives in an apartment just across the road from there," Frank answered sombrely, "I called in on her last week".

Sejal was trying to phone her sister, but all the lines were down, she was just getting the unobtainable tone. She was crying, not knowing what to do to relieve her worries.

I went into one of the meeting rooms to be met with the latest information, "The South Tower just collapsed, we just saw it happen", "Can't believe what I'm seeing".

I was annoyed that I hadn't seen the footage, it was incredible to think that a modern skyscraper could suffer this fate. As I watched the screen, I saw a tower collapsing. My immediate thought was that it was weird that they would replay this so soon, but I realised I was wrong. This wasn't the South Tower that I was watching, this was the North Tower.

"There's the other one going now!"

The room fell silent. Incomprehension hit us all. It was unimaginable what we had just witnessed. Sejal's sister – was she going to be OK? My mind was suddenly full of thoughts of this one stranger, someone I had never met, but perhaps it was better to focus on an individual plight rather than trying to process the overall picture.

By this time it was about 4pm. A message came through from the senior management team. It was one that showed great sympathy and I still remember the words - "In view of what has just happened in New York, we suggest that all staff leave the office now and return home to their loved ones. Hold them tight and savour every moment with them. If tomorrow morning you have any fears of travelling to, or coming to this office at all, please stay at home, we will understand".

I phoned Ian and arranged to meet up with him earlier than previously planned. His group had decided to go ahead with the evening's activities despite there being some qualms about being in a major capital city - what if there were copycats waiting over here? All flights had been grounded in response, so we felt safe. We did feel a little bit guilty enjoying ourselves, but there was nothing we could do about the developing situation thousands of miles away.

As we lay in bed that night I was grateful that I finally had a loved one to hold tightly, as instructed to do by senior management!

Friday 14 th September 2001

My aunt had died a couple of weeks before, and today was her cremation. I had arranged to drive my mum, sister and brother to Bournemouth for the family gathering and service.

It was an unusual occasion, as the person conducting the service referred several times to the large loss of life that had happened that week in America. Listening to his words I tried to work out whether the loss of a known elderly relative was a bigger deal than the deaths of thousands of unknown people. Was my feeling of personal sorrow worthy in a week when tragedy was felt globally?

Would my aunt have been angered that the service was not all about her? Why had God let all those people die? What was His purpose in all this? I cried anyway, unable to hold in my emotions at the end of a strange week.

Sunday 16th September 2001

This was the day that we flew to Athens. The previous few days had included several conversations about the safety of flying but we decided that at that moment it would be one of the best times to board an aeroplane, security had never been tighter and, more importantly, we would lose our money if we cancelled.

It was a tricky start to our holiday, as our flight, which was due to take off at 09.00 was delayed until 19.00, the plane had a technical problem. We had a fraught day at Gatwick and our late arrival into Athens meant that we lost a day of our cruise around Evia. However, it was a fantastic break and it was good to get away from the doom and gloom of the rolling news services.

Returning home and going back to work was very difficult for me. I had loved my week of freedom and I felt physically sick at the thought of returning to the job and the commute. Ian had already started talking about a possible change of jobs for himself in the New Year and he fancied one that would take him back to the Middle East. It was somewhere he had worked in the past and an opportunity was on the horizon.

Circumstances, or perhaps fate, intervened in October. One-2-One had recently been bought by T-Mobile, and the German parent company had instigated a corporate review. Strategic matters were discussed, every role was scrutinised and redundancies were on the table. It was a long process but eventually the results were conveyed to each department head and meetings were arranged.

It was apparently good news for me as my role and my tenure of that position was declared safe. My heart sank at this announcement. I knew in my heart that the best thing for me was to ask to be made redundant. Ian said he would support me in that decision and he would take me with him to Qatar, if the job materialised over there, so I would have to leave anyway sometime in the New Year.

Another member of the team, who was excellent at his job, had been told that he was going to lose his position. I took the plunge and went to my department head and offered to take the redundancy package that was on offer to the other staff member and then he could keep a role within the company that he loved working for.

This idea was discussed by everyone, and in the end it was accepted. On Friday 21st December, I boarded the train leaving Borehamwood station for the last time – I was free!

Monday 31st December 2001
We had flown out to America on Boxing Day, spending 3 nights in Las Vegas. What an interesting time we had there, but then we had moved on to San Francisco. After a busy day of doing everything a tourist should do in the city, we had booked a table at the 'Crab House' restaurant at Pier 39, overlooking San Francisco Bay. It was a special meal to celebrate the end of a year that had changed both our lives.

Sitting in that restaurant on that night, I looked back over the past 12 months and realised that I had achieved what I had thought was unachievable. My life had changed immeasurably and the future was a place that I looked forward to visiting.

In March 2002, Ian and I had a superb holiday in Japan, and then in June we moved to Doha where we sampled the ex-pat life on offer there for a short, but interesting 6 months period.

So 2001 was a momentous year for me personally, and also for the world at large. Writing this piece has highlighted those 12 months' true significance to me, and resurrected memories that no longer crossed my mind.

A moment's peace for Joyce in her husband's garden the 1950s

Rosemarie with her granddaughter in the 1970s

Jo with family in the 1960s

Maureen's carnival float with folding chimney. Poole 1976

Jocelyn with her children in the early 2000s

*Jude had to dress smartly for work
in the early 1970s*

*Carol at the office Christmas party
in the late 1990s*

4 FACING THE CHALLENGES

We all had challenges one way or another. Some were more problematic than others, but we have made decisions that we thought would suit us and our families.

Joyce   *1996*

One of the most exciting things I have done was to take part in Robin Knox Johnson's expedition. I became the most senior woman crew member in a 'Round-The-World Yacht Race'. I took part in one leg over six weeks. This obviously needed training and though I was still teaching dinghy sailing at South Cerney I would train for a year, mostly weekends, then join the race on its Honolulu to Hong Kong leg. This leg was stopping over in Japan.

Sir Robin said "Joyce is exactly the sort of person we are looking for, experience is not necessary but determination is."

The race began in London in October (1996). I can say I have sailed the Caribbean and Pacific oceans, traversed the Panama Canal, and, alas at night, spent Christmas on the Galapagos Islands. We had twenty eight days out of sight of land, standing regular four hour watches day and night. I have helmed the Clipper by moonlight, steered by the Southern Cross, seen whales, albatrosses, giant land turtles (George the giant tortoise was reputedly over 100 years old) and fed my breakfast to tame marine iguanas.

The going was tough in force nine gales, BORING in the drifting, drenching Doldrums, bruising and sick-inducing down below, but mostly exhilarating and magical.

Rosemarie   1973 to 2000

The initiative came from the then CEO for Gloucestershire to get a teaching workforce who had degrees. I had signed up to a degree course majoring in Primary School English and Educational Psychology. It meant lectures two evenings a week plus some weekends, all based in Cheltenham, plus assignments. It was a three-year course. Towards the end of the course I was appointed a Headteacher of a village school near Tetbury.

Fortunately Gloucestershire Education Authority paid for a set amount of supply cover prior to the final exams so I had time off to revise and finished my final dissertation. I took the last exam on my forty fifth birthday. I followed this with a part time science course for a diploma in primary science teaching. I now had the right pieces of paper but cannot objectively judge whether upgrading my qualifications made me a better teacher.

Local Heads who belonged to the NAHT met monthly. There was a thrust to each meeting e.g. employment law, computers in school. I was the President for a year. We met in the local Teachers' Centre which later closed on some cost cutting exercise. I had gained much from my meetings with other Heads. There were changes in education such as teaching science in primary schools. There was to be a National Curriculum. Parents committees raised funds for school. The working day was long.

There were evening classes available at Cirencester college. My husband went to a woodwork class and built a curved door for the main living room at home. The whole class came to a door hanging ceremony when it was finished. I went to learn about basic computing for use both in class and in school administration.

Before I retired the dreaded OFSTED inspections came online. Several colleagues took early retirement saying they would not have an inspector in their class. I was more stoical. By this time the numbers in the school where I was Head had trebled and conditions were crowded. Thanks to OFSTED this was noted, and the interior of the school was redesigned giving an upper floor and indoor lavatories.

My mother had poor health and in order for me to give some support to my father in caring for her, my parents moved to Poulton. The children went to Secondary School. They established their own friendship groups and educationally it was not convenient to make them change schools. I had always hoped to return to Surrey but circumstances were against me and I remain a Gloucestershire resident.

If asked I would say late 1950's and 1960's had most impact on my life, followed by 1970's and the move to Gloucestershire. By the 1990's one year ran into another and I was surprised when I came to write it up to find that quite a lot happened to me in the 1990's and there were significant changes. Strange what tricks memory plays.

Holidays.

My husband and I celebrated our thirtieth wedding anniversary in 1990. We planned to return to some of the places we had been to on our honeymoon, plus more. Wise now about the need to book concerts, et al for the Saltsburg Music Festival well in advance, in January 1990 we booked the main event of our choice, a performance of Don Giovanni, to be conducted by R. Muti, of whom I was a great fan at that time, and one or two concerts.

We started our trip by travelling on the Orient Express from London, joining the overnight train to Venice. It was a great experience with excellent food, attention to detail and perfect service. In St Anton visitors were allowed to board to take photos of a lounge area and I felt like royalty for a few minutes.

We stayed in Venice for a few days. We then had a hire car and drove to Saltzburg staying in the same hotel as 30 years earlier, then back via the places we had been to before.

During the 1990's we joined family members on holidays in Tenerife and later Brittany. We also had narrow boat holidays in the UK. We joined friends on their boat at Port Frejus and later stayed with them at their house in France. We had two holidays in Cyprus staying with friends who had been our neighbours in Poulton, for they had relocated there. A 'computer' colleague of my husband's and his wife entertained us at their French holiday home near Marseilles in two different places, as they changed location.

My husband, having left BAC when the Concorde project came to an end and before he retired, spent time in India working with Oxfam employees there. He took ten days' holiday and I flew out to join him just visiting Delhi, Agra and Jaipur. I loved the throngs on the railway platforms and the crowded streets, the bikes and three wheeled taxis. We travelled by private car with a driver. The sights such as the Tahj Mahal were unforgettable, especially the atmosphere, but for me the skinny lad washing down his water buffalo outside the Tahj was just as significant.

I played croquet on the hotel lawn in Delhi in a temperature of 40 degrees C. A Flunky kept us company, knew the game, and fetched the balls according to the rules so the players' efforts were reduced to as little as possible. I bought some jewellery and yes paid the tax at customs but at that time it was good value.

The hotels were a luxury and were built cheek by jowl with mud huts where people lived. We saw people sleeping on the streets, like London. The year after our visit a luxury tax was introduced so the visitors paid a lot more for the hotels. I hope the tax reached some of the needy. We kept to vegetarian food as my husband thought that the safest to eat.

We were in Seattle airport when we heard the news of Princess Diana's death. I think we were staging through on the way to the Galapagos Islands.

Snippets about the world at that time.

My son Huw worked for a company that made filters. There was a big growth in demand for environmental filters as public opinion swung that way. He travelled throughout Britain and could stop for a coffee or more often an early breakfast at roadside caravans where food was sold.

Police in cars had to catch a speeding motorist so the speed limit was often exceeded. Drivers sharp enough to keep a look out for the 'copcars' could maintain 90 miles an hour. There were not so many cars on the roads as now.

There was a growth in the use of mobile phones.

The National lottery began in 1994. Sport benefited and the UK gained more medals than erstwhile at Olympic level as competitors could be coached without great cost to them as individuals. Places of interest and historic buildings also benefited.

The Cricket Pavilion in Poulton was paid for by charity donations and a lottery grant kick-started that appeal. My husband, Poulton cricket club president, raised the money and project managed the build. Whilst the lottery was a drop in the ocean of the £450,000 needed the process was rigorous and once Sport England had approved a grant, other organisations donated.

My husband decided to retire in 1994 but I continued to work.

In school the National Curriculum became embedded. This included Primary School Science which began in the 1980s. I had gained a diploma in the teaching of Primary School Science, so was ready for the off! The children liked the subject perhaps because there was a practical element to the learning in contrast to the amount of 'pencil work' which they had to do in most subjects.

Computers came into use in the classroom. As mentioned I had been on a course prior to the start of this. The computers duly arrived but without plugs so the first challenge for me was correctly fitting a plug to each. Computer games were very popular in class but we did some simple programming too.

In April 1994 Huw's first baby, Stephen, arrived followed by Penny's daughter, Rebecca, in July 1994. Tim, Huw's second son, was born in March 1996 followed by Hannah in September 1997 and Penny's son, Chris, in November 1997. A sixth grandchild, Huw's daughter, Ellie, was born in 2000.

In 1998 I retired after eighteen and a half years as a Headteacher. I did invigilating GCSE exams at a local Secondary School and became a school governor at a local Primary School but not where I had worked.

I became a full-time housewife. I did most of the gardening, including caring for a large herbaceous border. My pride and joy was a sit-on mower. I looked after Chris some days while his mother was at work. I followed no plan but enjoyed the freedom each day brought.

I saw in 2000 at a Scottish Dance party. Laughable now is the threat of the time that computers would cease to work at midnight.

Jo   *1989 to 2000*

1989

We moved to Bolton. I must admit it was not my choice when it came down to it. However that is what we had agreed to do, and it was certainly a challenge! At the start we lived in a little terraced house, which would become our first student property, whilst we got to know the area.

All our furniture was piled up in boxes around us, most not even unpacked. This was late October. We had also brought our cat, Milly Molly Mandy with us. We did call her Milly for short, unless we were cross with her. We managed.

My sister Carole and Keith lived in a terraced house in the next road. We had bought another property the other side of Bolton and they had bought two, so the men set to doing them up ready to rent out to students as our source of income going forward.

Meanwhile we kept looking at properties and familiarising ourselves with the area. Carole and I then got ourselves jobs in local offices as temps. I did general office work in a large warehouse for a postal order company for a few months. It was OK but I did not feel as though I belonged there.

Frank's elder sister Irene lived nearer the centre of town with her daughter and we saw quite a bit of them.

1990

We were beginning to get used to Bolton. By this time we had three houses that we managed to let to students, Carole and Keith had four, so then we decided to look for our own home. One idea was to get a big house and share it. We went with them and looked at one but decided we did not want to do that. It was in a built-up area, on three floors, and did not have much garden. So they finally bought that for themselves, while we kept looking.

Then Irene, Frank's sister, found one near her, the first turning off her road. It had been built in the fifties by a builder in the style of the forties, as two semis. He had lived in one and sold the other. We liked it and could see the potential.

Meanwhile I got an interview for a part-time job at Bolton Town Hall. We had also booked a holiday. I got the job with Bolton Town Council and we were moving to our new home Devonshire Road and going for two weeks holiday all at the same time. I explained to my new boss and he said I could start when I got back from Hexham. I worked there for ten years, enjoyed it and made some good friends.

1992

We had settled in very well and now had two cats, Tutankhamun - practically a thoroughbred, a beautiful silver, long-haired Persian cross-breed, called Tootie for short. The second cat was Aggie; she was an ordinary mill worker-type of cat and we thought that name suited her! Tootie was a very disdainful and haughty cat!

I wanted to achieve something more intellectual so I went to evening classes and got three 'O' levels. Following through on this idea I researched Bolton Higher Education and Salford University and realised they were both doing degree courses that fitted in with my previous studies. Literature and Women's Studies seemed the most appropriate. After interviews at both places I then had to decide which one to take up as they both offered me a place. I accepted Bolton Technical College. The year I graduated it became Bolton University. So from September I was working mornings at the Town Hall and then three evenings (plus homework) at the College. I did enjoy it.

We had what was the dining room made into a large modern kitchen-diner. It was a lovely room with a big bay window. Then the smaller room leading to the garden became a more traditional dining room. Frank did the garden, laying a circular paving area halfway down, lawn and flower beds. It was lovely and we enjoyed the space.

Now that the student houses were done there was not so much work for Frank and Keith to do. Summer holidays were the busiest, re-decorating and getting ready for the next year's students. It is surprising how much mess the students could make - potentially a whole new book there.

1994

Golf became the most interesting thing for Frank, Carole and Keith. For instance, when we went to Wales for a fortnight, they had rounds of golf and I sat by the river through the golf course and read or studied.

1995

My degree took slightly longer because I started part time then went full time to get it finished. I graduated in 1995. I was not sure what to do once I graduated but was looking at doing a Master's, which I subsequently did, packing up my job at the Town Hall to complete my studies.

I was also attending a creative writing group, filling in a couple of times when our leader was away. During this time I took a course on teaching children writing, and went to a couple of schools to give lessons in creative writing. I also taught a short course run by the library for local children. This was interesting, but not for me; however I did have the qualifications if needed.

I carried on doing the Master's in Creative Writing so I achieved my MA in 1997. Then I started running my own Creative writing classes for the Workers Educational Association – the WEA. I ran five all over the area, Salford, Oldham, and of course Bolton.

The main problem for us was that we did not see our family enough. It was a heck of a drive up the M6 from Reading to Bolton. Then of course the grandchildren had started school so trips had to be in school holidays. We used to travel down to London to see my Mum and other members of the family occasionally, but were getting itchy feet for the south and our family.

1998

We had to travel down south for Frank's sister-in-law's funeral. It was good to have a family gathering but the circumstances – a funeral - not so good. However weddings and funerals became the only way we saw some members of the family.

1999

Like everyone else we were getting ready for the millennium. We had developed routines of gathering for a meal or outings with Carole and Keith, Irene and her daughter Christine with Doug her partner on most weekends.

This New Year it was going to be our turn. Doug volunteered to supply the fireworks and I cooked a special meal. The fireworks he bought were awful. Luckily as we were living at the top of the hill we were able to go out into the street and watch the fireworks from all over

Bolton. It was quite a fun evening. Doug was never allowed to forget his 'damp squids'.

There were all sorts of rumours running around of course about the Millennium Bug and we all waited to see what would happen! Then of course nothing did!

2000

So with the millennium came different ideas for our future. We decided to go back to our roots in the south for many reasons. We did still have a house down south that we had not lived in. We had been letting it out so it was paying its way with the mortgage, but we did have to wait for it to become empty, or their contract to end. Meanwhile we put our houses in Bolton up for sale. By late summer we had moved to a rented property the other side of Bolton. The owners were not such good landlords as us, but we knew it was just a temporary arrangement.

Maureen   *1984 to 2001*

This was a very turbulent period for me.

We had set up Gemma Microsystems together in 1983. One year on, things were not going well and by 1986 it was obvious we needed another source of income. I took a part-time job working for our accountant in his little shop in Fairford, but that was just an interim measure.

I began working for a civil engineering company based in Swindon. The IT department was very small, just four of us, the rest being men. We were working on live systems so it was very easy to erase a module accidentally, to the consternation of users! Fortunately this only happened to me once and I was able to retrieve the situation within a few minutes.

After about six months the Dutch owners of the company decided to move the headquarters to Reading. A few core managers were offered jobs there (though without compensation for either moving house or commuting). The rest of us were made redundant. This time I got a job in Cheltenham with a re-insurance company in the centre of town.

We had had four years of exams starting in 1983, with the children alternating. My daughter had applied to university but did not get the grades required so she took a job as a nanny, living in during the week but coming home at the weekends. The following year she got a place at a Polytechnic and my son qualified for a place at university. They were both due to leave home the same weekend.

We decided to bring forward my son's 18th birthday party to September. I did not know how I was going to manage my new job, the 25-mile drive to work and all the preparations for the party; the stress resulted in a slipped disc, the cure for which was strong pain killers and six weeks lying on my back on the floor. Although I had not finished my probationary period the company decided to give me sick pay and kept my job open.

For some years I was nervous of redundancy but everyone assured me that that had never happened at that company, they were good employers. I settled into a large IT department with a mix of men and women, eventually taking on the part-time role of Training Co-ordinator. This I particularly enjoyed, but it did bring me into conflict with the department manager who was known as someone who should not be crossed (nowadays he would be called a bully).

When it became fashionable to cut staff to the bone in the name of 'efficiency' and the CEO changed, the company followed everyone else. Despite reassurances from all my friends, my name was on the redundancy list again. I was devastated. Graham was still suffering from stress and earning nothing. Many people were taking early retirement at 50, so at 52 it was going be difficult for me to get another job. There was a real possibility that we would be on benefits for the rest of our lives and I was terrified.

I went completely to pieces and although I insisted on working my notice as the best way I knew of to recover, the only thing that really helped was the discovery that I could appeal the redundancy. I had a hearing, supported by my line manager, but lost. The next possibility was to go to an Industrial Tribunal. Graham consulted a Trade Union officer he knew, who told us we had no real hope of winning but could have our day in Court. We decided to go ahead, as representatives of so many powerless people.

In the meantime, after a number of interviews for jobs that were all unsatisfactory in one way or another, I was taken on by a small software engineering company based in Prestbury as a telephone support person. The pay just covered my travel costs and the mortgage but nothing else. The work was not ideal either but it was the best I could do.

I was working hard on the case in the evenings but at work I kept very quiet about the Tribunal as I felt it might jeopardise my position; people only found out about it from the local newspaper the day after the hearing.

Two of my previous managers were persuaded to be witnesses but to protect their own jobs they had to be summoned by the Tribunal. The company had engaged a Tribunal Chair from another district to represent them. He was obnoxious! We could not afford legal representation, so Graham acted for me. The panel was very lenient with us and tried to curb the barrister's bullying tactics. Even so he managed to spin it out so that we had to go back for another day.

When the time came for the verdict, I was almost sick with nerves. We knew we would not win but had hoped to score something. Sadly, something we had written in the first application, before we knew what we were doing, undermined our case and we got nothing (rather to the disgust of the Union rep on the panel). My erstwhile manager bounded up and insisted on shaking my hand. He did not yet know that he would be posted to Singapore to establish a Far East presence for the company!

After about a year in Telephone Support, I was given a chance to do some training for customers. We produced tools for Systems Analysts, based on the two (later three) different methods they used. For the training I had to get a basic understanding of these methods, something I had never been senior enough to do in my previous employment.

The company was expanding rapidly, usually by poaching employees from the place they had all worked originally. They were all young men and their background was engineering, unlike mine, which was Data Processing (office systems). Having reached the peak of what I could earn in Support I braced myself to apply to become one of the development engineers. They were happy to take me on and so I became the only woman developer for the next six or seven years. I was also the grandma of the organisation!

The work was really interesting, the best job I had ever had. Unfortunately, rapid expansion led to cash flow problems and we were bought out by an American company, then a British one. I avoided redundancy twice but finally the axe fell in 2001. I was nearly 62. I argued that I was thinking about retiring and persuaded them to let me work my notice until my birthday. I was able to walk out with my head held high and a contract for maintenance work in my pocket!

During the eighties my husband and I led a discussion group for teenagers from our church, meeting fortnightly in our home. The subjects ranged widely, no questions were barred, any opinion could be voiced and tested. The result was some fascinating and challenging discussions that left us talking long after the young folk had gone home. It was a formative experience for all of us.

I was also teaching in Sunday School, when in 1990 I received a flyer for a diocesan course in Children's Ministry. I was interested, thinking that it would expand the work I was doing, possibly into other local parish churches. My children, when consulted, said, "Go for it!" so I applied and was accepted. The end result of the course was to be licensed as a Reader in Children's Ministry. I had no idea what an ordinary Reader was or did, but that did not worry me as this was clearly something different.

We were a group of ten women and two men, all of whom had the backing of our local churches and vicars. A thirteenth was withdrawn from the course when her vicar found out that the lady would have full Reader status and he thought she was only suitable to work with children(!).

We soon found that this attitude was not uncommon. There had been considerable opposition to the establishment of the course because it was felt that anyone could do children's work; no special training was needed, certainly not to the high standard required of Readers. It was even thought by some that we would be debasing the title. It soon became clear that we would have to outperform the other trainees if we were to be accepted.

When the course began, I found that half of the modules we were following were common with the traditional Readers' course and half were specialised. I enjoyed the challenge of returning to academic thinking, albeit in such a different sphere. However, during the second year of training I was made redundant and I went to pieces. There was talk of my having to leave the ministry course because of my mental state, which to some indicated my unsuitability for any parish role. Fortunately, there were other more sympathetic people around and I was allowed to continue.

By this time, I had discovered that Readers were expected to get up into a pulpit and preach. I said, "Over my dead body!" but was firmly told that it was an essential part of the course. I acquiesced and said to myself "Just this once".

We had to write the text of a sermon which would be marked by a bishop before we were to deliver it in our placement churches. The subject was St. Thomas who is famous for having doubts. I have never subscribed to the opinion that doubt is the opposite of faith, so I wrote about the positive benefits of a faith that is tested by doubt. The bishop approved it and I braced myself to get up into a pulpit – for the one and only time.

After the service a woman spoke to me privately saying that I would never know how much that sermon had meant to her. To say I was astonished is an understatement. I felt I had nothing to say to the world but if the world saw it differently, then I had to go on. That is how I came to preach regularly in my own and other churches for the next twenty-five years.

Somehow it always seemed to be my turn to preach after the most shattering of events. The Sunday following the Dunblane massacre of Primary School children and their teacher was Mothering Sunday. How could we celebrate mothers when so many families were shocked and grieving? I could only speak from the heart and pray that I was speaking to the heart of others.

Again, following the unbelievable event now known as 9/11, I was due to preach on the Sunday. The Christian countries of the West were being forced to acknowledge the power of Islam to inspire reverse Crusaders. Leading Church thinkers began to take this 'new' religion seriously. In the meantime, there was no possibility of ignoring such a momentous event, but how could anyone begin to make sense of it in a matter of days? Yet people needed to hear words of sanity…..

I never gave up working with children, though I saw the originally intended special licence for Children's Ministry become just one clause by the time we were licensed. Not long afterwards the clause was dropped altogether "because everyone should be doing it anyway". How much of this stems from lack of understanding of children's spirituality and how much from lack of respect for roles traditionally filled by women would be hard to say.

In 1988 Graham's mother, no longer wanting to live a two-hour drive from any of her children, came to live in Fairford. She had been suffering from arthritis and had a hip replacement, which unfortunately went wrong. It became infected and had to be removed and she became wheelchair bound. She died from a stroke in 1986 whilst Graham and I were on holiday in Tenerife with the children and two of their friends, one being Heidi who is now my daughter-in-law. (The holiday was one of those special offers given to people who withstood an evening of hard selling by time-share companies.)

The following year my stepmother died. My father carried on living alone, but eventually it became clear that he needed to go into a home. Although it was one he knew well, he never settled and he too died in 1999, having just passed his 90th birthday.

My sister, who lived in Barkingside, had been suffering from severe depression. It was obvious that she needed more support than Social Services could offer, so we persuaded her to move to Fairford. Despite her problems, she was beginning to recover and settle here when, with no prior warning, she too died.

The Millennium passed without a Bug, as I felt sure it would – for well over a decade work had been going on to adapt computer systems in large companies.

In 2001 I was retired and for the first time in many years we had no dependents.

Jude   *1989 to 2004*

My middle years between the ages of 45 and 60 are not something I would want particularly to remember, nor to re-visit. They were filled with dramatic events I would rather forget but maybe by skirting over the worst times I can confront some of them as a catharsis.

In 1989 I was 45 and two years into running my own law firm, now based at 218 Strand, opposite the Royal Courts of Justice, specialising in High Court personal injury and medical negligence cases, construction and intellectual property law. I was sharing premises with Hillearys another law firm I had met in Temple Chambers.

In 1989 too, we gave a splendid summer party on the back lawns, with a live jazz band and wonderful outside catering. That was a high spot I remember fondly.

In 1990 I took in two partners who over the next 4 years set about defrauding me, causing much distress. Basically, they were running two separate firms under the same name, one taking all the profit and the other all the liabilities. I only discovered when two tax demands were received with differing reference numbers. Investigations ensued.

In 1994, now aged 50, I moved in with Bull & Bull at 199 Piccadilly where I spent the next 8 years. My husband's firm had spectacularly imploded in 1995 leaving all equity partners (of which he was one) in serious multi-million-pound debt to the bank- Child & Co, who were also my firm's bankers. We became the bank's problem. Unable to make us bankrupt, which would have meant the end of our being able to practice, they allowed us to continue.

Having always vowed we would never work together, he joined me as a partner in the practice in 1996. To cut a long story short, the next 14 years were extremely difficult. His practice loans were secured on our house which was in negative equity. Repaying the bank became a daily living nightmare.

Sophie our elder daughter had won various scholarships and out of the three had chosen Malvern Girl's College. She played national lacrosse there and ended up being head of house. Camilla followed her there in 1992, but in 1994 both girls left - Sophie for the V1th Form at Haberdasher Askes and Camilla for South Hampstead High School which gave her a bursary to help ends meet.

In 1996 Sophie went up to Edinburgh to read history but after six weeks asked the Dean to be released from her course of studies and came home. She wanted to read law. At Edinburgh she could either do international or Scottish law, for the former needing an A level foreign language which she did not have. She spent a year working in various shops and re-applied ending up at UCL.

We finally gave up having a live-in nanny/housekeeper in 1996.

Camilla went up to Bristol to read Theology and Religious studies in or about 1999, later undertaking a post grad degree in Marketing at Imperial. In between she acquired some sort of diploma in the wine trade while at Justerini Brooks where she was PA to the Chairman.

It wasn't all doom and gloom. We managed all of us to go ski-ing for quite a few of those years and to have several holidays abroad. My husband was a governor of the local Primary School and I was not only on Deanery Synod for Hampstead but also on Area Synod for the local sub-diocese. We had dinner parties and enjoyed going to the theatre and concerts.

We worked 24/7. Going into the office for daily 12 hour stretches including weekends was normal. It became a way of life. The nature of the practice had entirely changed with my husband coming into it. It now specialised in high value commercial property and property-related commercial law. Our clients were in the main of high net worth, many international. I was now undertaking company sell-outs, mergers and acquisitions and restructuring, leveraged finance and the like. Any litigation of course was undertaken by me. And I did all the infrastructure work such as the accounts etc. We increased our staff level to around 12 at any one time.

Our hard work paid off. The firm prospered and eventually we were able to pay off the bank.

In 2002 we moved premises to 6, Gray's Inn Square where we spent the next 15 years. The practice really took off when there, and in 2004 with me turning 60 we were both able to breathe a sigh of relief and to start living a life again, despite all the setbacks and financial woes, of which there were many more that I have not related here.

And during these years the world saw :
1989 The Berlin Wall coming down
1990 Iraq invading Kuwait
1991 Gorbachev resigning as Soviet President
1992 Charles & Diana separating
1993 Text messaging between mobile phones being launched
1994 Black holes being discovered
1995 Israel prime minister Rabin being killed
1996 The outbreak of Mad Cow disease

1997 Princess Diana being killed

1998 Google being launched on the World Wide Web

1999 The beginning of the needless Y2K scare

2000 The human genome sequence being deciphered

2001 Twin Towers in New York being hit by terrorist planes and destroyed

2002 PC sales topping the £1 Billon mark

2003 Space shuttle Columbia exploding and killing all 7 astronauts on board

2004 Facebook being launched.

Jocelyn   *2006 to 2015*

When we moved back to the Bristol region we purchased a house in Chew Stoke, a village just south of Bristol.

Work itself was very exciting; by 2006 I had several educational research projects on the use of new technologies on the go and was beginning to have my work published regularly.

One project that I am particularly proud of comprised online teaching resources that linked science with ethical questions to promote discussion that are still in use today: www. beep.ac.uk for biology and www. peep.ac.uk for physics. We were about to create the chemistry version when education had one of its periodical somersaults, the government supported ideals and the funding behind them changed and it was shelved.

The day job involving visiting schools and student teachers across the region was still 24/7 at times and, during term-time, I was kept busy. My favourite time of year though was the end-of-the-summer project work and out-of-school teaching, making rockets on the Downs and studying forces in play parks.

We were again fortunate to find a child minder whose took our youngest two in as company for her own children and the older two, doing GCSEs and A levels respectively, were now well able to manage for themselves. Both Rod and I worked in areas where, a lot of the time, we could organise our own schedules and, with our new PCs, work from home, so family life with all the associated children's ills and spills continued to be managed without too much trouble. Woe betide anyone who forgot to update the giant year planner in the study though.

With a steady income, family holidays changed to feature further away destinations. We still went camping in North Devon every year with my friends from university yet also, over time, visited several of the Canary Islands. Fuerteventura was a favourite as it had both quiet sandy coves for the younger ones and, on the other side of the island, waves for the older ones.

My decision to buy everyone a family ski-ing holiday for Christmas 2008 though did not go down at all well. All the children were resentful that they had only mini-stockings and Rod, after falling over a few times, refused to go back after the first lesson. However, as adults these days (well, apart from Rod) they are all keen to accompany me ski-ing, should I offer to pay their way.

Busy with work and family life, national and international events largely passed us by. The 7/7 bombs in London in 2005 made little impact, we were much more closely focused on when the next Harry Potter book would come out. Indeed when Harry Potter and the Deathly Hallows, the 7th and final book in the series, was published at midnight in 2007, my eldest daughter and I were in the bookshop queue.

In 2008 she was awarded her degree in Engineering from Cambridge which made my father's day for he, too, qualified as an engineer at Cambridge, indeed she found him in a group photo on the department wall.

It is now that I have to admit that earlier I skipped a significant chunk of my history for, when doing my PhD at Surrey University, following an attack of flu, I suffered vertigo for weeks and, after an unpleasant series of tests to identify potential triggers, was diagnosed with Menière's disease in one ear. An operation was unsuccessful and left me partially deaf. However, I quickly learned ways to live with this, the associated tinnitus and the occasional giddiness.

However, in 2011 I discovered it had been masking another problem. I went to the doctor as I was worried I wasn't coping as well as usual and following an MRI was diagnosed with an acoustic neuroma, a benign tumour on the acoustic nerve of my healthy ear. If ever there are three people in the room when you are given the results of a scan, be prepared for bad news. The tumour was the size of a tangerine and the medical team were surprised by my calm reaction, I just wanted it out as soon as possible.

The operation went well but left me severely deaf. Work colleagues were amazingly generous, I had the biggest bunch of flowers I had ever seen and it was only recently that I discovered how worried the family had been.

After recuperating I went back to work and was able to change my role to spend less time in schools where hearing was an issue and more with the international students who brought in a significant chunk of the university Education department's income. These were qualified teachers from a wide range of countries who came to Bristol to study for Master's and Doctorate degrees.

However, over the next few years there was a range of pressures for us to deal with including unpleasant accusations from the Education Secretary, Mr Gove, for many academics did not support his latest reforms. There were also financial challenges as the number of students wishing to train as teachers dropped. Even the promise of huge bursaries could not persuade graduates to teach Physics and, when I asked them about this, I was informed that the amount of money offered made them think something must be very wrong in schools.

University lecturers were up in arms over various pay and funding issues and there were several one-day strikes which we were pleased to see were supported by the students too. On a protest march we all filled Park St in Bristol only to be charged by half a dozen mounted police, a seriously overwhelming sight and sound which made us feel more important than we likely were. However, despite everything, the Education Department was still looking to downsize and in 2015 I was asked if I would take early retirement.

Carol   *1991 to 2000*

In July 1991, I had relocated to London and was living back at home with my mum. I started my new job in August and everything was on track for a positive future – apart from one thing, my body was not happy.

My problem had initially been treated as a bit of a joke, by myself and my friends. A few weeks before my 30th birthday in May, my left big toe had become very swollen, inflamed and painful. The 'experts' in the office immediately diagnosed gout, due to my high consumption levels of red wine. I was compared to King Henry the Eighth, "see what good living does to you"!

My first concern was the pain, but a close second was the fact that I was unable to comply with the unwritten rule (or perhaps it was written), concerning appropriate office attire within the WH Smith head office. I could no longer wear the obligatory high heeled shoes – my foot could only bear being put into a comfortable training shoe. There was much debate among the higher management about the best decision for my feet, as I really couldn't be in the office if they forced me to wear 'office' footwear. Finally it was decided that I could wear trainers, and, in a first for my department, I was allowed to wear trousers too, as training shoes teamed with a smart dress or skirt really was an unbelievable sight.

My GP was unable to work out what was really behind my issue as several tests had revealed nothing to give her any clues. As the weeks went on, the inflammation moved into most of my other toes, so at least my left big toe didn't feel on its own anymore!

I managed the issue with pain killers when necessary and up until September I got on with my life the best I

222

could. However, one day, on a day off from my new job, my cat was being naughty, so I knelt down on my right knee to retrieve her from under the armchair – something, I wasn't sure what, went in my knee. There was immediate discomfort and as the afternoon progressed, it started to swell up. By 7 o'clock I was sitting in the A & E department of the local hospital and later that evening, I had my first experience of having the fluid drained from my knee – it was a very long needle, and not pleasant, but at least afterwards I could bend my knee again.

So now my knee had joined the 'pain party' that was beginning to creep around my lower joints – next it was my ankles and walking became increasingly more difficult. One of the good things about the company I now worked for, was that they had a more relaxed approach and they were happy for me to wear what made me feel comfortable in the office – so no more stupid shoes or business suits, which was a relief.

After relocating to London and initially staying with my mum, I realised that I preferred having my own space and started looking for a house to buy. I was lucky to find a property I could afford. It was quite a brave thing to do, as I was under pressure in my new job as my health issues weren't in keeping with the young, vibrant image they were trying to promote. My boss at the time actually told me that she was fed up with the sales representatives that came to the office to see us, always asking how I was getting on and showing concern for me.

I felt that I had to hide my problem and pretend nothing was happening, and I also felt let down by the 'sisterhood' and the lack of support that a fellow female was giving me. Luckily she was soon recalled to America to take up a senior role within the company and a more sympathetic leader, a man, came on board.

Now living in south London, I was referred to a consultant who was one of the country's leading authorities on arthritis and together we embarked on a journey of experiments over the next few years. The main problem we had was there was no tangible reason why this was happening. Nothing showed in any of the numerous tests I had, which included cardiograms and a particularly unpleasant fasting regime.

I spent a week in the Royal London Homeopathic Hospital having all sorts of natural substances being laid or injected into my body, but nothing really showed itself as a cause or remedy – I was an enigma! I spent quite a bit of time on homeopathic remedies, as my consultant really didn't want to put me on steroids at such a young age, but they only helped to a certain degree.

I tried a series of visits to an acupuncturist, but this only seemed to make my pain worse. I have memories of leaving the hospital in Great Ormond Street and struggling on the tube to get myself back to Colliers Wood, where I was living – I couldn't quite accept that any treatment should make your problem feel so much worse, rather than better!

The really interesting bit about my problem was that it then developed a routine which baffled everyone even more. It seemed that every 10 days my joints would become very inflamed, I would feel it building inside me. Each episode would last around 48 hours during which it felt like I had the worst bout of 'flu ever, in addition to the painful joints, and then it would settle down again.

The only good thing about this was that I was now on a timetable that meant I could start to plan my life around the good times. I knew which days in the coming weeks I would be unable to walk properly so avoided accepting invitations for social events. On bad days I just went to work, did my best, and then straight home to bed exhausted from the effort of it all.

My colleagues at work were excellent and did their best to help me. I would get myself up the stairs on arrival in the morning; this sometimes took me ages as each step was agony, and then at the top, one of them would have my office chair waiting for me – it was on wheels so I could propel myself around from that point, although sometimes I got pushed. They made me my cups of coffee etc, and the only time I had to walk anywhere was to go into the toilet. I must have been a real grump at times as it was very frustrating to feel so useless.

I had regular appointments with the consultant and he was very sympathetic to my situation. I remember an occasion when I had been invited to the Brit awards ceremony but I knew it would be on a day when my knee would be swollen. He arranged for me to go to the hospital on the morning of that event and have my knee drained and have cortisone injected into it, so that I could manage to go – 'Cinderella, you shall go to the ball!'

I do believe that I was a bit of a 'lab rat' for him, as he suggested we try many different treatments, some of which I can't actually remember now. I know I had weekly gold injections which made me feel important for a while, but that can lead to problems with your kidneys, so I had to go and have weekly blood and urine tests too.

My boss was a very tolerant man, as I spent a lot of time out of the office attending appointments but I always made sure I did my work when I was there and feeling 100%.

Another theory was proposed that because there was this '10 day' pattern in my health, that it might have something to do with my own body's 'clock', particularly my menstrual cycle. I was put on the contraceptive pill and I was told to 'play' with the natural order of things. Sometimes I would take the pill for just one week and then stop, and other times I would continue to take the pill after the 3 week pack was used up, trying to jolt my body out of the rhythm that it might have entered, causing this issue. So I would go weeks without a normal bleed and I think, again, this caused me more problems than it resolved, as the experiment proved to be a failure. I think that this may have contributed to me experiencing a very early but prolonged menopause, although it is just my opinion.

After a couple of years of treatment and with no improvement in sight, I decided that while I was still able to walk reasonably well, for at least 7 days in a two week period, I needed to push myself to do things that I might regret missing out on in the future. The doctors were unsure how the disease would develop and how long it would be before it spread into other joints – the prospect of being in a wheelchair at 40 was often discussed!

I bravely researched and booked myself several holidays. I had decided to go on my own as I wanted to be in a position where I could decide for myself how much I was capable of doing each day, and going alone meant that I wouldn't spoil the experience for anybody else. I went to Malta first and then challenged myself with a Nile cruise and then a coach trip around the Peloponnese in Greece. I had an interest in ancient sites so these were perfect for me.

My final jaunt on my own took me to Venice and I have fond memories of the day I went to the small island of Baveno. My legs were very bad that day but it was the last opportunity I would have to go, so I forced myself. I must have presented an interesting sight. As it was a hot day, I wore shorts that revealed various layers of tubigrip bandages that shrouded my legs. It must have looked strange to the locals.

My progress was very slow and painful, so much so that a very elderly lady, who was standing outside her house, called over to me and insisted that I took a seat with her. She couldn't speak English and my Italian was very poor, but she expressed to me how sad she was to see me struggling, so we shared a glass of lemon drink and a special moment of bonding between 2 physically impaired women, divided in age by about 50 years!

My foreign holidays then changed into family affairs. I travelled with my mum, sister and brother for a few happy trips. The timing of these holidays was fixed by the fact that my brother was a teacher, so I couldn't work them around my 'good leg times' so much, as it had to be during the half term break. It was good to have their support and encouragement, and sometimes I probably did more walking than I would have done if I was on my own.

My biggest memories come from the week we spent in Sorrento. What a beautiful place it is, but a town built on a hillside, which means walking up and down inclines – picturesque but painful. One day we went on a day trip, which started with a visit to Mount Vesuvius. The coach took us up quite a way, but the final ascent to the top was to be on foot. Oh My, that was a torture for me. My brother was willing me on, insisting that I shouldn't give up as I was so close to the top, but I knew that what goes up has to come down, so every step up was soon to be replicated by another step down. I did it and was able to look into the crater of the volcano that was responsible for the destruction of nearby Pompeii – which was our next destination.

I was so looking forward to seeing all that Pompeii had to offer, but my earlier 'hike' up a volcano was now limiting my ability to carry my own body weight around. The guide apparently gave an impressive tour, all of which I missed because it took me so long to get from each point at which she stopped to give her explanation, that by the time I caught up with the group again she was moving on to the next place – very frustrating indeed. My visit to Pompeii turned into a disappointing 'trudge'.

I was filled with a great deal of despair that evening and remember standing on a small precipice overlooking the coastline below Sorrento and considering that if I threw myself off into the valley below, I probably wouldn't feel any more pain than I was momentarily feeling and that if I did break all the bones in my legs and feet in the fall, then at least I might get replacement ones, that in time would make me better – yes really that's what I thought!

In the middle of the decade, I was prescribed a drug called Methotrexate. This was a particularly difficult phase for me, as the side effects were very nasty. It was a drug that I could only take at the weekend, as it often meant I was ill with nausea and headaches for 48 hours after I took it. My Friday evening started with the hesitant taking of the thing that I dreaded and then I just coped with the consequences.

Some weeks weren't so bad and I was able to do a few things like shopping, but other times I felt 'yuk' the whole weekend; bed was the only place I wanted to be! One such weekend in August 1997, I lay in bed late on a Saturday night watching the TV when I was shocked out of my slumber by the news reports coming through that Princess

Diana had been injured, and then killed, in a car crash in Paris. I found this very difficult to accept, as since she had arrived on the scene in 1981, I had felt a connection with her, but it was only because we were born in the same year.

Finally in 1998, I was transferred to a different hospital and a new consultant. She spent a lot of time with me, reviewing the history of my treatments. She was flabbergasted that I hadn't been offered the chance to use steroids, as it was her view that some of the other things I had taken and done, were perhaps doing more harm to my constitution than they would. That was when I started on the steroids and my story gradually changed. Yes, they did make my face change shape, but really that was the only negative I could report. The inflammation, the episodes of pain, diminished and it was a wonderful release for me.

Over a period of 2 years, I carefully reduced the amount of steroids I was taking and eventually I found that I didn't need to take them anymore. My joints stopped swelling – it seemed to be a miracle – whatever my body had been reacting against, was gone.

Looking back on the decade where I was meant to be '30 and flirty', in reality, it turned out to be a complete disaster. What man in his right mind would want to hook up with a woman who couldn't walk half the time, had to wear the most un-sexy things on her legs to support her joints and spent most weekends feeling exhausted and ill? I just didn't spend any time on that aspect of my life, which has been a big regret for me.

Of course, my dream in 1991, had been to find a man, settle down and create my own family, but that wasn't to be. At the turn of the millennium I had to be content with the fact that I had made it through the most challenging years of my life, with my sanity intact and my zest for life renewed.

Joyce (1996) crewing in the Round the World Yacht Race

Rosemarie birdwatching

Jo receiving her degree

*Maureen licensed as
a Reader in the 1990s*

*Carol at a crab restaurant
in San Francisco, 2001*

*Jude with family
at a wedding*

*Jocelyn at work in the
2010s*

5 COMING INTO OUR OWN – THE RETIREMENT YEARS

Some of us have finished! However, others have had longer lives and are still going strong, well, still going anyway. Of course we have the Pandemic to contend with. We older ones have had our four jabs and keep wearing our masks and are hopefully getting through it. I think on the whole we are still apprehensive but we escaped the millennium bug 21 years ago. Although the pandemic has been with us for two years now, things seem to be getting easier.

Joyce   *1990s*

In the nineteen nineties my husband was offered a very good position in Cirencester, so we moved from Rugby. We have lived in Poulton ever since in the same bungalow.

Now that we are on our own we have the occasional lodger. We joined a group that provides accommodation for students. At the moment we have two very pleasant young ladies. One is a returnee who, having lived with us before, has come back to her old room.

I was one of the founder members of the u3a in Fairford, and it pleases me to see it still going on.

A course I started with the u3a was called 'Dancing to Five Rhythms'. I found my body responding with pleasure to the five rhythms and it was very liberating. We began with flowing music, then staccato and chaos. We followed on from that with a lyrical piece and rounded off with a gentle meditative piece into stillness. Some of the music was pop, some classical, some folk. We were 'Dancing the Wave'.

Dancing alone, without partner or organised steps, ignoring the other dancers and letting ourselves go, required confidence and a lack of self- consciousness which did not suit everyone, but those who stayed loved it. A friend and I introduced the concept to our local u3a and we have a flourishing group of dancers who still meet at the local hall once a month.

Also at this time I started the sailing club, which I led for two years until I had to stop because arthritis stepped in.

Rosemarie   *2000 to the present*

With no family responsibilities we went on a number of holidays which I preferred to call experiences or adventures for few were relaxing. We went to unusual places.

The longest trip was six and a half weeks on a repositioning cruise on a converted Russian trawler with just sixty passengers. It had a strengthened hull built for Antarctic waters. It also had a large roll capability.

We boarded at Ushuaia and travelled south to have three landings on the Antarctic peninsula. We went through storms in one of which the hull got dented at the front. We were allowed on the bridge and I found watching the gale and experiencing the roll wildly exciting.

The lifeboats were like sardine cans and fortunately we had just one practice at getting in and out of one.

Having left the Antarctic peninsula, we visited islands on the way back finally leaving the vessel at Cape Verde.

Other holidays included two trips to Siberia, Machu Picchu, circumnavigation of Svalbard where we saw polar bears, China where we followed part of the silk route, The Azores, South Africa and others. I rode a camel in the Gobi desert when I was seventy.

My husband liked Norway as he had a friend there and we went several times including our last holiday together which was on the Hurtigruten where we saw the Northern Lights. By that time my husband was in the last stages of terminal cancer.

I was widowed in 2012. I continued with hobbies some of which I had enjoyed with my husband. I played croquet, mahjong, belonged to the WI, was a church flower arranger, school governor and joined the u3a. I was a member of a Scottish Dance group and went birdwatching.

My husband had been President of Poulton Cricket Club and I was honoured to be asked to take his place after he died. This has remained a great interest. I am particularly proud of all the youth work done there.

Holidays were with my son and his family or my daughter and her family. Other holidays were either on my own or with a college friend. We chose coach trips within the UK. I went on some bird watching holidays in the UK with a company called Island Ventures. As everyone had a similar interest being on my own was no problem.

I stayed in the family home but as it was of genuine Cotswold Stone construction finding suitable qualified maintenance people was a challenge. After three years on my own I started house hunting and ended up buying on an estate in Cirencester. The house in Poulton sold within three weeks. I moved in October 2015, 44 years after buying the house in Poulton. I was close enough to keep up my interests in Fairford as well as those in Poulton.

Covid eventually restricted my hobbies though I learned Zoom to continue with the Creative Writing Group and WI.

My youngest grandchild is now 20 the eldest two 27. I am truly blessed to have them whilst my son and daughter have been and still are a great support.

Jo   *2000 to the present*

2000

I was still running several W.E.A. Creative Writing groups in the area - Bolton, Salford, Oldham, to name a few. I planned to continue teaching with the WEA when we moved south.

We were ready to go by early in the new year, March, earlier than we'd thought. With the two cats in baskets, which we took straight down to their new home, Frank and I went and stayed the night with Fred and Sheila in their bungalow ten minutes' drive away. We returned to our house by 8.30am to find the removal men on the doorstep.

It was an eventful year. Mum died just a few days later, 17th March, four days before her 82nd birthday, so we had to go up to Chingford where we stayed with Heather, my younger sister, and Graham to help with organising the funeral and clearing the small rented flat where Mother lived. Then we went back to our new house in Barton on Sea to unpack some more. Then we travelled back again to Buckhurst Hill for the actual service on the 25th of March.

A lady came up to me at the funeral and introduced herself, we had actually gone to school together! I did not recognise her or her maiden name at all. But she mentioned some of the other girls we'd known, so it was definitely an old school friend. We still write and phone each other two or three times a year.

Anyway back to the new house in Barton on Sea. We could walk to the beach from that house and it was comfortable for the two of us and the cats. We had a small extension built at the front to house a downstairs loo and the flat front window from the living room we had made into a big bay. After a few months we wanted a conservatory to finish it off. We got some quotes and organised it for September.

2001

Come September the weather was good, as I remember, and the men were OK so on the Tuesday Frank and I went for a walk after lunch. We told the men that, "We'll be gone about an hour Bill", and left them to it. When we got back after our walk, Bill said "I think you ought to switch the box on".

We could not at first understand what was going on - was it a science fiction film, a horror movie or just some weird scenario somewhere? Then the voice-over was telling us what was happening in New York. Then another plane dived straight at the tower! It was really unbelievable. We saw and heard sirens going, buildings collapsing, even ambulances and the crews being caught in the explosions.

It was so shocking it was difficult to comprehend the disaster. The hundreds of workers being killed if not by the actual planes then by being stuck in these tall buildings. Flames roaring out of the broken windows, people jumping from tremendous heights. It must have been a quicker death than burning alive. It was horrendous and made worse by the fact it was actually happening at that moment. It was hard to believe.

Later, in 2014, I went to America with my daughter and we went to the two towers site. It was amazing. Two huge fountains and all the names of those who had died engraved in the sides. Lots of people, but silence, as we all took in the huge number of names. It was awe inspiring.

I got in touch with the local W.E.A. (the Workers Education Association), in Southampton to organise some creative writing workshops in the area. I managed to get some groups going in the local community centre and in a school at Christchurch. I also ran a group from a student's home in Hythe and a meeting hall in Southampton. These last two groups I worked with until I moved to the Cotswolds in 2015.

2003
We had a lovely New Year at Alcester, a big Georgian house beautifully decorated, Carole and Keith, Sheila and Fred and us.

There was a big family wedding in Chigwell. My sister Heather's son Ben was marrying Jo, from a Greek-Cypriot family. One of the interesting traditions from there was pinning bank notes to the bride's dress. We spent a very pleasant couple of days with Heather.

2004
The following new year Pauline and Ken joined us all at Alcester as well.

2005
Pauline, Frank's sister, died in the following March. We had visited them a few times while she was ill. It was terrible to see her deteriorate; it must have been worse for Ken.

2006
Because of Frank's worsening health we did start thinking about moving. We liked the area but the house with stairs was beginning to get hard for him. On our walk down to the beach, we had seen some lovely flats that were a little different from the usual square blocks. If we had to move, that would be the place. These were privately rented flats that were gradually being sold on the open market. We found a flat on the ground floor. There were

two blocks, two floors, eight flats in each block. The flat had two bedrooms, two bathrooms and someone else to cut the lawns! We had a small patio area and a couple of small areas we could cultivate. It suited us well.

2008

This was a great year! Our golden wedding anniversary took place and my grandson Simon and Emma got married.

We celebrated our Golden Wedding Anniversary with a big family event at the Lyndhurst Hotel in July. About fifty family members came along. Most stayed at the hotel for two nights. Some just came for the Saturday, coming early morning and going home Sunday. On the Saturday I organised a trip into the New Forest with a picnic and games after a long walk. Then in the evening we all gathered for a meal and music and dancing. We even had some speeches.

Emma and Simon's wedding was at Congleton near Manchester. They booked the event at one of these modern wedding venues where the ceremony, meal and party all happened in the same place. It was a lovely family event and there again we had to stay over. It all went very well.

2011

Frank's health was deteriorating. I came home from work one lunch time and the ambulance was there. They took him to hospital. He was there a week or two then home again, but was not well. In July I had to call the ambulance again. I followed on by car as the ambulance took him to Bournemouth hospital. He was there for a couple of weeks, then he went to Christchurch Hospital for the weekend, then was transferred to Lymington Hospital.

I packed up work and spent most of the days at the hospitals. Then after a few months they said there was nothing more they could do, so they suggested a nursing home. He was transferred there on the Wednesday and died on the Saturday. I went back to work the two days, at Southampton and Hythe.

2013

My daughter, Joanna, and Ray had moved to Fairford and finally persuaded me that I also should move there. I had been travelling to them every month or so to visit and quite liked the place but was using a lot of petrol. I liked where I lived but have always enjoyed the excitement of moving house. My son Martin and Alison also moved, to Ludgershall which was just an hour away from Fairford. So after a lot of humming and hawing I put the flat up for sale and warned my creative writing classes that I was thinking of moving.

2015

In March I had a buyer and was frantically looking for a new home in Fairford. If you are moving to the Cotswolds you want a stone cottage, don't you? Well I did. However after looking at a great many I ended up with a 1960's bungalow! Everything was finally working out, moving dates were settled, and I sold loads of my big furniture, mostly on e-bay.

During this time I developed terrible headaches. I had never had such a bad and prolonged headache, so I went to the doctor's after a few days. I could not see my own doctor, so I saw a pleasant young man who examined me and sent me to a physiotherapist in Lyndhurst. It was just four weeks until I was due to move and also go on holiday with my daughter and son-on-law. The physiotherapist organised sessions twice a week and seemed to cure my head.

Frank's sister June, who lived in Devon, died on the second of June (her birthday was the third). The funeral was on the fifteenth of June and I was moving on the seventeenth, then going on holiday on the twentieth. Fred and Sheila drove down to Devon on the Sunday but I had an excuse to wait until driving myself down Monday morning. Finally I moved house on the Wednesday. Martin came down to help me at that end and when we arrived in Fairford Joanna and Ray were there, and Simon also came to help. It was beautiful weather to move, however we had to get ready for an early start Saturday morning to fly to America.

Then something strange happened at the airport, I could not push the trolley straight, I just kept turning left without meaning to – very odd. Still, we got underway and went to Long Island near New York for a few days to get our breath back, then we started travelling around America. But I think I was in a bit of a mood, and felt strangely unwell. We saw the house where Walt Whitman was born and had an interesting tour by local students. But after a few days Joanna and Ray took me to a local clinic, when we should have been seeing West Point. From here on in I have no recollection of events, just what I have since gleaned.

I was then taken by ambulance to a hospital in Newburgh. After a few days I was released with medication and told to rest, so Ray and Joanna took me on to our next stopping place, a lovely house in Ithaca. But from there I became worse and collapsed. I was then taken by ambulance to Syracuse Upstate University Hospital an hour away and operated on twice because they found out I was suffering from multiple strokes.

I was in the hospital for three weeks. Joanna and Ray had to cancel the rest of their holiday and book into a hotel near the hospital. The hospital was wonderful. I sometimes wonder what would have happened to me if I had still been in Gloucestershire. We finally came home with a private nurse, flying from Canada with me, Joanna and the nurse in first class and poor Ray having to travel, just behind the curtain, in economy class, luckily all paid by the Insurance Company.

I stayed with Joanna and Ray for about a month and then finally moved into my bungalow.

My sister-in-law Jean died in January 2016; she had been ill for some time. She and Don, Frank's youngest brother, had lived in Essex for many years so of course it was another long journey to attend the funeral. Joanna and I went. It was in February. It was a long drive there and back in one day. There seemed to have been a lot of funerals, still I felt more and more glad that I had been in America when I needed attention.

By this time I had joined the u3a as a committee member and facilitator of the Creative Writing Group and was making lots of friends amongst the members.

2017
Joanna and I travelled to Essex again this year to see Don and he also came and stayed with me for a few weeks. Another funeral this year. The next brother, Fred, who we were quite close to, died and we had the journey down to Highcliffe for that. This was where my husband's ashes were so we utilised the journey to visit his memorial.

2018

Another funeral. Don had never got over Jean's death after nursing her for about a year and he finally died. Also in this year I had another trip to Washington DC, now in my eighties, when my great-granddaughter Raina was born. It was a premature birth and she was in the hospital for a few weeks. But we managed to see her several times. My grandson was horrified to learn that, as the quotes for my travel insurance for the trip had been so high, I had bought a reduced package. It still cost more than the flight, and did not cover me for existing complaints – any further strokes. But it was worth it!

2019

The last real Stichbury died. Not quite reaching her century, Irene was nearly 99, a wonderful lady who had been in the WRAF during the war, meeting the man who became her husband. They married in Egypt and, living in Bolton, she was quite an influence on our lives actually. I went up there by train for the funeral and stayed a few days with Christine, Irene's daughter. Then Christine and Doug, her partner, brought me home and stayed with me for about a week.

2020

The Pandemic! Isolation! I was so lucky having my daughter living nearby, as she had to organise shopping for me. We got through the first year, but it was a funny quiet Christmas that year.

2021

We had our vaccinations, the first one for me on seventh of January. I had the booster on thirteenth of October. Things are gradually easing this year. I am still wary of mixing with unknown people, but I organised a Christmas lunch for the Solos group where I seem to be the leader. I am now also running the Beginners' Table Tennis group, along with the Creative Writing group.

Maureen   *2001 to the present*

As a retirement project my husband and I decided to try and visit the places on the continent that featured in the paintings of his great-great-grandfather. By profession J.J. Dodd taught architectural drawing at Manchester School of Architecture. Unknowingly his granddaughter went to the same school as a young woman, studying for three years but stopping short of taking her final exams. The qualification was of no use to her because she was about to get married and middle-class women did not work in the 1930s.

JJ was the younger brother of a professional water colour artist. He himself was untrained though a few paintings are to be found in art galleries around North Wales and he left a number to his family. The best are architectural, not surprisingly.

We visited Caen and found the church that he had painted, then the next year we stayed in Toledo and found the spot in the cathedral where he must have sat. It was interesting to note the features he had omitted for the composition.

Unfortunately we later learned from a guidebook in Bangor Museum that he had probably painted from lithographs, apparently a common practice in Victorian times. It is unlikely that he had ever visited the sites so our enthusiasm for the retirement project waned.

In 2004 we celebrated our 40th wedding anniversary. We had taken out shares in my previous company when it floated in America. These were now pretty worthless but we decided to cash them in anyway. Conversion fees would have eaten up a significant chunk of the money so the obvious solution was to celebrate our anniversary by going to America, drawing the money, visiting Graham's godson in Florida and making a six-week tour of the States – at least it was obvious to Graham! Frankly, even I did not think it would happen until the tickets were booked a month before we were due to go.

We made the most of what we knew would be our only visit there, sleeping in motels as cheaply as possible, eating rather a lot of pizzas because they were cheap and readily available, and mostly stopping wherever we had reached by the end of the day.

We started in Boston where, excited and jet-lagged, I tripped and broke two fingers, thus wasting a day in hospital having the fractures treated. I just about made it to a concert of the Boston Symphony before we set off on a roundabout route to Niagara Falls. From there we tracked back towards the coast and drove down towards Florida, taking in Colonial Williamsburg and the Blue Mountains on the way.

Driving through Georgia we saw fields of cotton ready for picking. Before her marriage and again for a couple of years before my brother was born, my mother worked as a six-loom weaver in a Lancashire cotton mill. On occasions my sister and I had to go in to see her at work. It was a frightening place, incredibly noisy, with huge overhead leather drive belts in constant motion and picking sticks flying backwards and forwards at great speed. Now I was seeing the source of all the cotton, making a connection I had never imagined.

From Florida, where Graham's godson lived, we hopped over to Las Vegas to see the Grand Canyon then drove to the West coast, ending at San Francisco. It was the adventure of a lifetime.

On returning home we settled into a quiet life filled with church and u3a activities. To family members Graham's memory was obviously failing and he eventually diagnosed with mild Alzheimer's. Other medical problems meant that he became less and less active though he loved going out for short trips, preferably somewhere local where we had not been before and with a coffee shop. I began to take over our finances and the driving.

In 2018 he died in his sleep. It was not unexpected and it was the best possible time and the best possible way for him. One month later I went into hospital for a hip replacement and spent the next year getting back to full fitness. I took up Italian and, daring or foolhardy, not having done any ballet before, I signed up to Seniors' Ballet classes.

The following summer I went on a river cruise through Provence with my daughter. We had never holidayed together before but it was a resounding success, despite the worst heat-wave France had ever experienced. We had the time of our lives. We were due to go together to Oberammergau in 2020, but, as everyone knows, the world was engulfed by Covid19 and like everyone else I have spent most of the last year in lockdown and communicating by Zoom. All of which has given me time to write the story of my life.

Jocelyn   *2015 to the present*

Being encouraged to take early retirement was a bit of a shock to the system but there was always plenty to do. We had recently purchased a narrowboat with the money Rod's dad left to us; travelling the canals in it took up several weeks of school holiday each year. During term time there was the busy schedule necessary to keep our youngest two, now teenagers, fully occupied as they took turns to take their GCSEs and A levels.

Their older brother was often at home, jobs for graduates had become very few and far between and he struggled to earn enough to pay rent on a place of his own. His older sister though was busy at work in a myriad of different locations around the world as she had joined the RAF.

I also joined several local groups such as the Village Art Group and tackled Spanish and Creative Writing with the u3a. What with my usual commitment to tennis twice a week, I now seriously question how I ever found time to go to work.

In late 2016 we became grandparents as my oldest daughter presented us with William; he was born a few weeks early and I went to stay in the special care baby unit to help support them both. I am very grateful to the charities that fund the rooms for visitors there. It is now 2021 and I am pleased to report that William is a vigorous soon to be 5 year old now living with his parents in New Zealand.

Over the last few years we have moved the narrowboat to different marinas, discovering in the process we preferred rivers to canals. We ended up in the marina at

Lechlade on Thames and, when Rod retired in 2020, we moved to the town to be closer to the boat.

We now have a small house in a 'retirement community' yet struggle with the idea of having reached a later stage in life. Between us we volunteer for the local hospital's League of Friends, the library, the Cotswold Canal Trust and the Wikimedia Foundation. However, I have always prioritised time to follow Creative Writing with the u3a and can now proudly say that I have received my first rejection for my 'would be' novel. Who knows where this collection of women's life stories will lead us?

Carol   *2002 to the present*

We had been in Doha, Qatar, for a few months over the latter part of 2002. In December, we were planning our return to the UK for the Christmas break when Ian was informed that he was no longer required on the project he was working on. So that meant our time in the Middle East was over.

One of his colleagues, who lived in a company-rented villa with us, had been telling us about a house he owned in Normandy and what a beautiful area it was. We had previously both expressed an interest in having a house in a foreign country, so this we pursued, finding a property to purchase near Vire. It was a large wooden chalet style house with a huge garden which included a substantial pond, so big that we called it 'the lake'!

It was a strange purchase process, as the couple who were selling it were getting divorced and they didn't want the sale to complete until July 2003, but they allowed us to move in in the February, once we had paid the deposit required under French law. So for 5 months we stayed in it regularly, furnishing it and started developments to the garden, but we hadn't actually paid for it.

One of the failings of this adventure was our lack of knowledge of the French language. I had achieved an O-Level Grade B but the intervening 25 years had drained most of what I had previously known from my brain. We muddled along and the estate agent we had dealt with became a handy translator when we needed help – he must have thought we were slightly mad.

The most bizarre event happened one weekend when we were there, there was a knock on the door. We opened it to an elderly man who started talking in very quick

French – I explained we didn't understand him (I had got very good at "Je ne comprends pas"!) Gradually it became clear that he was the mayor of the town and we had failed to do what was normal in France – apparently when you move into a new area, the first thing you are expected to do, is to visit the mayor's office and introduce yourself to him or her. We hadn't done that, so he had come to us.

He sat down on our sofa and, armed with my Collins dictionary, we took it in turns to point at relevant words and used hand gestures to fill in the blanks. After a few painful minutes, he made the decision to give up, wished us well and promptly left, never to be seen again!

Ian was lucky to get a new consultancy position working on a project that would see him splitting his time between London, Reading and Immingham, in North East Lincolnshire. I remained in my house near Colliers Wood and he did the commuting from there, staying in Travelodges near Immingham when he needed to be up there. As the year progressed it became apparent that the focus of his efforts was going to be in that location, so we decided to rent a cottage near the plant. The London house was not really suiting our needs anymore, as when we weren't 'up North', we tended to want to be in France, so in October 2003 I decided to sell the house I had owned since 1992. The profit I made on that was extremely welcome!

We continued to rent in North East Lincolnshire for the short term and then Ian's time on that particular project came to an end. This was in December 2003 and we were already booked on a post-Christmas trip to Orlando. I had never experienced the delights of Walt Disney's extensive theme parks so like a little kid, I was excited to have the opportunity to pretend I was 8 again!

We made a big decision while we were there – we had been dithering about where and how to 'tie the knot', so we agreed to be spontaneous and ended up getting married at the Orlando City Hall on New Year's Eve. Just the two of us and the officiator. I did shed a tear as I thought of my dad and how I would have loved him to walk me down the aisle of a beautiful church, but at this stage in my life, I was happy to be with the man I loved, committing our lives to each other – in rather a sterile way, in an office really, but we had done it nevertheless. We married at 9.30am, then went to the local IHOP (International House of Pancakes) and then on to the Kennedy Space Centre for a very interesting and educational day – not very romantic but perfect for us!

On returning from America, we immediately went to France for a short visit. We then needed to decide where we wanted to live. As Ian was out of work, we could have stayed in France, but we were scared of our language inadequacies and I didn't fancy living there permanently, although looking back it would have made the most sense.

After a long period of house and location hunting, we found a property in a setting that was acceptable, so we moved to near Spalding in Lincolnshire. We loved the house and the open space around it, surrounded by farmers' fields, and not a lot else. Unfortunately we hadn't done our research properly and being so remote didn't really suit our way of life and we sometimes felt that we were stuck in the middle of nowhere. Fate also stepped in, when on the day we took possession of the house, Ian started a new job in Great Yarmouth which was a horrible 2-hour drive away, so it turned out that he needed to stay away from home during the week, which made our decision to buy the house almost redundant.

After owning the French house for just over a year, we realised that we wouldn't really be able to use it properly. We had tried the experiment and it had failed for us. We were lucky to make a decent profit on our investment so that made us happier about it all.

After a year in Great Yarmouth, Ian was off to Aberdeen for another job, so that's where we went for about 9 months, renting a nice house in Cove. While I was up there, I got myself a part-time job working as a buyer for the Grampian Fire and Rescue Service, which was an interesting change of use of my skills. That few weeks of employment turned out to be the only work I have done since leaving T-Mobile in December 2001.

In Spring 2006, Ian was on the move again, this time to Ploiesti in Romania. I remained behind in England initially, until he had established himself and decided that it was somewhere he wanted to stay. He found an apartment to rent in a communist style tower block, so that's where we lived for the next two and a half years.

It was an interesting time for us both and it was a real eye-opener to live in a country that was finally coming out of the heavy shadow of the Communist era, and also being there when they joined the European Union on 1 January 2007.

Ian had a lot of influence on the project he was working on and made sure that the people he employed were paid higher wages than they would have previously expected to receive. He had to be careful not to upset too many people with his capitalist approach but his staff were happy to have their brand new company cars, laptops and inflated salaries – they were very loyal to him, as you can imagine.

As 2008 came to a close, so did Ian's involvement in that project, so we returned to our lonely house in Lincolnshire. Ian had worked extremely hard in Romania, giving up weekends to get ahead with his tasks, thus earning money seven days a week. When we got back home, he decided he could afford to take a few months off – so it was holiday and gardening time.

In our travels around the National Trust properties of England, I had seen many gardens that gave me inspiration for how I wanted ours to look. It was a blank canvas really, so needed a plan. We decided that Ian would create our own version of what I dreamed of and he set to work. It took a long time, but we eventually had a garden that fulfilled our requirements.

Ian took on a few more work projects over the next few years as he said he needed a rest from the hard physical toil I was making him do! The best one came in May 2012, when he accepted a role that took us to Paris. We had 7 fabulous months in a wonderful city. I was so lucky to have everything that such a great city has to offer on my doorstep and while he was at work I took the opportunity to do all the sightseeing I could fit in.

I bought a membership to The Louvre and visited there most weeks, and still don't think that I managed to see everything in their collection. It was perfect for me as I could wander around at my own slow pace. My other favourite places were the several cemeteries, which on a sunny day offered a walk with added interest, as it was fun to hunt out the graves of the famous people whose last resting places these were and marvel at their intricate headstones. We made our last journey back from Paris just before Christmas. We still hadn't bothered to learn to speak better French, but it didn't seem to matter.

A few more short contracts followed for Ian, but in the main, we have been able to become 'people of leisure'. We reviewed our assets and future pension incomes and this gave us the security to decide that work wasn't a necessity. If we were careful with our expenditure then we had enough money to last us. We know we were very lucky to have reached our goal at such a young age and sometimes we feel guilty – but our own previous hard work, shrewd investments and thrift had got us to this point. We worked out a budget which enabled us to treat ourselves to occasional holidays, always making sure we got the best value for our money.

Once more in life I was aware that I needed to get around the world while I was healthy enough to do it, scared that my earlier mobility issues would reappear and spoil my plans. Cruising has become our favourite type of vacation and over the past few years we have been to some fabulous places, including lots of countries on our wish list.

I cannot list them all but the highlights would have to include the time we sailed across the South Atlantic in early 2016 visiting many fascinating ports of call, going down the east coast of South America, including Rio, Buenos Aires and the Falkland Islands. Later on in 2016, we crossed the Atlantic again, but this time northwards and then along the St Lawrence river in Canada, to visit Montreal and Quebec. Other memorable trips include those to Greenland, Iceland, Hong Kong, Singapore, Sydney, Auckland, and so many more.

Apart from the cruises, the other special holiday we had was a tour of China, where we visited Shanghai, Beijing and The Great Wall, and, thinking about it, it also included a cruise down the Yangtze River. I have particularly special memories from our visit to the

Chengdu Panda Research Base and seeing the tiny, newly born panda cubs in their 'cots', it was enough to bring tears to my eyes.

After owning the house in Lincolnshire for many years, during which it was often just the place where our furniture lived, we decided to look for a new location to live in, somewhere a bit more 'handy'. The closest shop to us was three and a half miles away along country lanes, one of the pitfalls of living in the countryside.

We started to look for a location which had the amenities we required within easy walking distance. I had always wanted to move back to the north Swindon area as it was somewhere I had enjoyed living in the 1980s. At the end of 2016 we purchased one of the show homes on the new estate on the edge of Fairford. We couldn't move into it immediately as we rented it back to Bovis so that they had an example to show their potential customers what they were offering. We waited until February 2019 for it to be ready to receive us as its new occupants. I felt like I had finally 'come home' and loved living in such a great little town with such a good community spirit.

We had always fancied playing bowls, so eventually joined the Fairford Bowls club, and I joined the u3a, participating in both the Creative Writing and Book Circle groups. However our plans hit the buffers when several issues came to a head in 2020, including Covid-19. The details don't matter in this account, it's enough to say that it meant that with a heavy heart we moved away from Fairford in January 2021.

Now living in Derbyshire, once more in a rented property, we have to make the difficult decision on what our future will bring. Where will we end up? Will we find a location where we want to settle permanently or are we destined to be forever wandering? Only time will tell.

Joyce exploring Venice in 2012

Rosemarie on holiday recently

Jo visiting Spain (2017)

Maureen sees where cotton comes from (Georgia, 2004)

Jude skiing in Tignes

Jocelyn (2019) at the helm of her narrowboat

Carol visits the Falklands in 2016

6 REFLECTIONS

We are coming to the end of our stories. No, not the end, just up to date with them. Some of us refused to let this be called a conclusion, that sounds too final. Although with covid19 causing us all to be isolated and have vaccinations who knows….

Joyce

I have lived a full and at times exciting life. My ambition now is to get a little motor scooter! My children, although very supportive in most ways, are not really helping me in this regard!

Rosemarie

My philosophy is that there is nothing to be gained from looking back and dwelling on the 'should I or shouldn't I' have done something. Even so I do look back at times. Should I have returned to work full time? Certainly my children had to learn to be independent. Once they were at Secondary School they had lunch money but if they chose to make sandwiches and keep the money that was their choice. I never made sandwiches not did I make their beds. They had to help at home too. Those are examples of how my chosen lifestyle affected them. Being at work meant I missed their sports days, school plays and concerts in which they were taking part. I had not been happy as a stay-at-home Mum and sought the stimulus of a career. I could build an argument on the 'fors' and 'againsts' of the decision I made.

When retirement came I had no plans. For my sixtieth birthday I was given a glider flying lesson. It was magical but I thought at the time I was too old to learn to fly a glider so did not take it up. Twenty four years on I think I should have had those lessons.

A positive in post-work years was that I had many interests and enjoyed the freedom of deciding each day how I would fill my time. I had time to be out and about with my husband and more time to meet friends, often for meals out. I learned new skills such as making mosaics in glass, mostly of birds, and there were the many holidays already mentioned. My husband liked to celebrate his birthday and each year in May we had a weekend house party for the six grandchildren and their parents. It was invariably sunny. Those were great times and valuable, for the grandchildren are now building lives for themselves and getting a date to suit all is difficult.

As a family we had a week together in North Wales for my seventieth birthday. We did have a family break, five nights in London together staying in Browns hotel, to celebrate my husband and I being married fifty years. I was a widow when we all met up in Bath for a weekend staying in a MacDonalds hotel for my eightieth birthday.

I have twelve champagne flutes from Murano bought when my husband and I went to Venice. They have decorative gilding. They have to be washed by hand. When my husband was alive that job fell to me and I was terrified I would break one. Now they are carefully wrapped and no longer see the light of day.

Other mementoes are stored away: a book of farm animals given me by my grandmother when I was four, another book that was a school prize when I was seven, a box containing the head-dress that held on my veil when I got married. It had been worn by my mother and later by my daughter. There are more things too. It is the small things, large ones, and some I deem important ones, that build into a lifetime of memories.

Looking back at my working life I recall that I was always in the playground at the end of a school day, often with a list of parents I wanted to chat to and they were very supportive, helping their child with use of capitals, story writing, more reading practice, suggestions that were well received, thankfully.

Headteachers were an elitist group of their own making when I was appointed. I therefore swelled with pride on my appointment. I took a turn at supervising playtime as there was always an adult in the playground when the children were outside. The same applied at lunch time but even when I was not on duty I watched and listened to the children at play. It is an ideal time to learn about their likes, dislikes, friendships and so on.

A fun story: A group of girls was setting the scene to play schools. One was to be the Infant teacher, one the secretary, one or two to teach Juniors and so on. One young lass said, "Well what am I then? You haven't given me a part." The others looked nonplussed briefly then one said, "You can be the Headteacher". "No" came the quick reply. "'Coz she wouldn't do much would she?"

I reserve judgement on my life. Did I do much or did that child put in a nutshell my use of the years I have had? Suffice it to say many blessings have come my way. I have much to be thankful for and must hold on to that thought as old age brings its challenges.

Jo

It has been a long and eventful life with plenty of ups and downs for myself and all mankind, with world disasters, family crises, happy times and sad times. Looking back, I wonder where the time has gone. I am now eighty four but still feel sixteen, no perhaps in all honesty thirty six?

It is now nice that I am friends with my children, not necessarily a parent. Mind you, they are more likely to treat me as their child! No really, Joanna and Ray will hopefully be popping off to America to see Alek and his family. We see Simon, their eldest, and his family quite often. So Joanna and Ray's children are doing well and I shall be pleased to see them when they pop over next year. Of Martin and Alison's three, Alistair is married and works for Barclays Bank, Cameron is at Teacher Training College and Naomi is studying and hopes to work with horses. I do wish their Grandfather was still here to see how all our grandchildren are progressing and doing so well. Then of course there is the next generation, our Great Grandchildren, Elliot in Bristol and Raina and Caretta in Washington DC; who knows where they will end up?

Maureen

Social historians tell us that the twentieth century was one of great change, especially for women. Our stories tell how the changes affected the lives of a few women born around the middle of the century, the detail that makes up this bigger picture. Some changes came from outside, like improvements in health care and educational opportunities. Other changes we were instrumental in making happen simply because of the times in which we were born.

It has been interesting to look back and see how a few ordinary women who were 'just getting on with their lives' embraced the opportunities presented to them, whether in education, work or home life. Some things we had to fight for; other things were the result of the work of previous generations of women, and some men. We are not superwomen, but examples of how small battles won can help to win the war.

In some ways we have been pioneers, though we may not have seen it that way. From a time when a few women decided that they wanted to work outside the home, it has nowadays come to be expected of them. Two-income households are in most cases essential for a mortgage and single-parent households (the vast majority of them led by women) are told that the way out of poverty is to work. The process of childbirth has been transformed from a medical event into a social one in which the mother has agency and choice. Marriage is no longer seen as the primary goal and a bad marriage is no longer a life sentence.

We have seen the strength of ordinary women facing up to difficulties and how they use the experience to become ever more resilient. We take things in our stride.

We embrace new opportunities, we accept change, we adapt. Even in later life we remain intellectually curious, prepared to take on new challenges. Belonging to a demographic that is not expected to be 'tech savvy', that is assumed to be content to do things the way we have always done them, in less than a week from being told that we must go into lockdown for at least three months, our group was assembling on-line and exercising our creative muscles just as before. Maybe it is our long experience of coping with whatever life throws at us that enabled us to do this.

Jude

I have only written a fraction of my life story. Some of the best bits have been omitted because of not fitting in with the rest of the life-stories in this book, or because they were considered to be of scant interest to anybody else, or because I simply have not had the time, or the timely recollection, to recount them. That is a pity, but never mind. Comparing notes with my fellow contributors, I am aware that my life has perhaps been 'unusual'. But has it? All of us have in some way had privileges and all of us in some way have been disadvantaged in terms of stable and loving childhoods, education, health, opportunities, abilities and relationships.

My life has been one big adventure which has not yet stopped. I am 78 going on 29 and ready for the next chapter whatever that may be, I start with the advantage of a happy marriage, a loving family, my own home, no pressing financial worries and reasonably good health. How I got here is a source of some wonder. The past is now just a story to be read in the context of the times and I hope with amusement.

Jocelyn

What things have changed?

Looking back there have been key changes since I was a small child in the 1960s, these include the national currency and the rate of inflation which increased dramatically throughout my teens but is now at historic low. Yet more apparent to me are the changes in the way we cool or heat our houses and store food. Refrigerators were huge, expensive and an American fad in the 1960s and it wasn't until we moved to Singapore that we had one. This meant that food could not be stored for long and it was usual to go shopping nearly every day. These days though people rarely visit their local high street, the towns are much quieter except at weekends and many shops have folded. Many villages are now without even a pub let alone a shop. As for heating, central heating rather than individual fires that need to be laid and lit each morning is now the norm and, when you visit a tropical country like Singapore, most buildings are air conditioned rather than cooled with the rather erratic fans we used to have.

Along with the explosion in information technology, video games and ever-increasing ways of watching television, this has led to a massive increase in the amount of electricity we all use. I have become very aware of the need to look at the bigger picture. How is that electricity generated? Will it be sustainable?

Other concerns of mine, highlighted by the changes I have seen on beaches and when snorkelling, are in the materials we use for packaging and clothes. Plastic litter has become a feature of any holiday trip and I am pleased to see that now supermarkets are making a conscious effort to reduce their use of plastic.

It is interesting to have lived through the heyday of plastic, generated from crude oil. It was touted as a wonder material and became increasingly prevalent. My children's toys: doll's houses, racetracks, kites, skateboard wheels and even their clothes: easy-care fleeces and trainers are all largely manufactured from different plastic compounds yet my toy farm and its animals were wooden and, for most of the year, we were dressed in wool with leather Start Rite shoes.

I recognise that I have been very fortunate to have experienced the past 60 years from the perspective of someone who lives in a developed country, whose parents had a more than adequate income, whose further education was funded by a government grant and who, themselves, soon found employment whenever she sought it. My partner and I were able to buy a house before the age of 30 but, these days, with graduate unemployment and heavy student loans, I see my children struggle and I can see why they are reluctant to save.

On the plus side, there have been notable advances in medicine and health care. I have a BCG scar where I was vaccinated for smallpox but none of my children do, for smallpox itself has been eradicated globally since I was a child. In the 1960s I had weeks off school with measles, both German and the ordinary type, but the MMR has made these diseases rare. Perhaps though, we got overconfident for, as I write this, we are coming up to the end of a second year where everyday life has been massively affected by the Covid-19 pandemic.

Carol

Writing my life story over the last few months, I have spent a lot of time thinking back, and putting events down in 'black and white' has reminded me of many things and emotions that perhaps I had forgotten, or at least not thought about for ages. In my mind, the majority of my recent reminiscing has probably been viewed through very rose-tinted glasses. Was my life up to this point so great, or as time passes, do the hardships lose their significance?

I think it is difficult to look back and review every important, or even insignificant, decision you have made and proclaim which ones were wrong and which ones were correct. The fact is that one will never know what the opposite decision would have created, there is no script for the alternative narrative for each potential 'sliding door' moment, where two scenarios would be able to play out side by side, but what a fascinating concept that is.

I feel that I was fortunate to have been born when I was, where I was and into my family. I don't remember ever being told I wasn't able or capable of doing anything I chose to do. My school education was good enough to get me to university and no-one ever discouraged my ambition – I was even encouraged to apply to an Oxford college, but that was not to be. I was just a normal girl from a working-class family but I had the privilege of achieving my dreams. How lucky was I?

I feel a great deal of gratitude to all the women in the previous three generations who had pushed against the barriers that held them back, as they built the strong foundations on which my life was built. I don't believe I ever felt discriminated against because of my sex, apart from knowing that my salary was less than my male colleagues for some periods of my career, although we were doing the same role, but that didn't matter to me at the time - I was content.

I have tried to view all of my experiences through the perspective of the time that they happened, as I don't believe there is any real benefit in being outraged with the help of hindsight. The sexist language in the workplace in the late 80s was laughed off, and dealing with male salesmen who each had their own unique view of women, I accepted at the time, but can see now that they should have been questioned. They didn't affect me then and didn't hold me back. I was probably guilty of using my feminine wiles to gain an advantage sometimes.

Luckily I never got sucked into the darker side of the 'sex, drugs and rock 'n' roll' lifestyle that surrounded me at certain work events I attended - drugs never tempted me and I am grateful for that.

The world has changed so much during my lifetime and technology has taken over much of everyday life, some with better consequences than others. Looking back, I enjoyed the challenges that presented themselves when computers weren't around, a time when you had to work things out for yourself. I think relying on computer-generated data would have made my working life more mundane, removing the skills that I developed and that I am still proud of.

However, my university studies would have been a lot easier with a laptop that would have given me access to lots of online research, negating numerous visits to venerable libraries in various locations, and it would have been a pleasure to have typed out my essays rather than using my trusted ballpoint pen. My hand aches after writing a few lines now!

I have played the Mark Twain quote, "Twenty years from now, you will be more disappointed by the things you didn't do than by the ones you did do", over and over in my head, so what does that mean to me at this point in my life? Perhaps because I am still here, alive and happy, I should report that I have no regrets, but that isn't true.

My biggest disappointment is not having children. I have always felt this was not my decision, or perhaps that's what I have told myself. I have learnt to accept the fact that fate stepped in at the very moment I believe that chapter of my life was going to happen, throwing health issues my way that only cleared up too late. On the flip side of that, the life I have lived over the past 20 years has been amazing, full of adventures and experiences that I would have missed out on if I had fulfilled my other ambition. So to Mark Twain, I say "No!"

An important thought just occurred to me. This time next year, I will be the same age as my dad was when he died - 61 and a half. So looking forward, I have to push on and live my life to the full, enjoy the stage of life that he never got to experience. At 60, I guess, and hope, that I am only two thirds through my time on this earth – which when I think about it is exciting, worrying and breathtaking, all at the same time!

So in summary, I believe my 60 years have been (to paraphrase Lemony Snicket) – 'a series of FORTUNATE events' – with much more to come!

THE END

Printed in Great Britain
by Amazon